Candle in the *Wind*

Sharmishtha Shenoy is an accomplished author known for her contribution to mystery and crime fiction. She has authored the compelling true crime novel *The Hyderabad Heist*, published by Rupa Publications.

Sharmishtha's popular and acclaimed Vikram Rana mystery series includes titles such as *Vikram Rana Investigates*, *A Season for Dying*, *Behind the Scenes*, *Fatal Fallout*, *Silent Witness*, *A Thousand Scars: Book One – The Hunter*, and *A Thousand Scars: Book Two – The Hunted*. She has also published a short story collection titled *Quirky Tales*, and a standalone thriller, *Murder in the Chowdhury Palace*.

Readers can explore her blogs at www.sharmishthashenoy.com or contact her directly at sharmishtha.shenoy@gmail.com.

Candle in the *Wind*

STORIES OF TRUE CRIME AGAINST WOMEN AND CHILDREN

SHARMISHTHA SHENOY

Published by
Rupa Publications India Pvt. Ltd 2025
7/16, Ansari Road, Daryaganj
New Delhi 110002

Sales centres:
Bengaluru Chennai Hyderabad
Jaipur Kathmandu Kolkata
Mumbai Prayagraj

Copyright © Sharmishtha Shenoy 2025

The views and opinions expressed in this book are the author's own and the facts are as reported by her; these have been verified to the extent possible, and the publishers are not in any way liable for the same.

All rights reserved.
No part of this publication may be reproduced, transmitted or stored in a retrieval system, in any form or by any means, electronic, mechanical, photocopying, recording or otherwise, without the prior permission of the publisher.

P-ISBN: 978-93-7003-694-9
E-ISBN: 978-93-7003-158-6

First impression 2025

10 9 8 7 6 5 4 3 2 1

The moral right of the author has been asserted.

Printed in India

This book is sold subject to the condition that it shall not, by way of trade or otherwise, be lent, resold, hired out or otherwise circulated, without the publisher's prior consent, in any form of binding or cover other than that in which it is published.

To all the strong women who have enriched my life:

Nandita Mukherjee, Mondira Sarkar,
Rita Dutta and Saroj Jaiswal

Contents

Foreword / ix

The Kidnapping of Baby Ishitha / 1

Innocence Robbed / 45

Unrequited Love / 67

In the Name of the Children / 118

I Will Never Let You Go / 152

Foreword

When I embarked on a career in law enforcement, little did I know that my path would lead me on a journey filled with heartbreaking stories of female victims. Over the years, I have witnessed the indomitable spirit of these women and their unwavering determination to seek justice. It is with great humility and a heavy heart that I write the Foreword for Sharmishtha Shenoy's *Candle in the Wind*, which was inspired by true crimes against women and chronicles some of the cases that have touched my life.

True crime narratives have the power to shed light on the darkest recesses of our society, to expose the vulnerabilities that exist and demand our attention. In this collection of stories, we explore the lives of women who have faced unimaginable trials, whose voices were silenced but whose stories deserve to be heard.

Throughout my career, I have had the privilege of working alongside incredibly dedicated detectives, forensic experts and advocates who have fought tirelessly to ensure justice for these victims. I have witnessed the pain etched on their faces as they stood in courtrooms, fighting for justice on behalf of those who could no longer speak for themselves. It is their unwavering commitment to the pursuit of truth that has inspired me every day.

As a female Additional Director General of Police, and as Head, Women's Safety Wing, Telangana Police, I understand the unique challenges faced by women in our society. These challenges, unfortunately, extend into the realm of crime. The stories in this book highlight the complex interplay between gender, power and violence, reminding us of the urgent need for societal change.

To the victims and their families who entrusted their stories to be shared in these pages, I am deeply grateful for your courage. Your resilience in the face of unimaginable tragedy serves as a reminder that we must never falter in our pursuit of justice. Your stories are not just statistics or sensational headlines; they are reminders of the lives that were lost and the lives that could have been. It is our collective responsibility to ensure that their legacies are honoured and that their stories are told with compassion, empathy and respect.

To the readers, I implore you to approach these stories with an open mind and a willingness to confront uncomfortable truths. Only through understanding and acknowledging the realities faced by these victims can we hope to effect change. Let their voices echo in your hearts and minds, inspiring you to become advocates for justice, champions for those who have been silenced.

It is my sincere hope that *Candle in the Wind* will serve as a catalyst for meaningful conversations, as a call to action for reform, and as a tribute to the resilience of the human spirit. Together, let us work towards a society where no woman's voice goes unheard, where justice is a reality, and where these stories of pain and loss become lessons that propel us towards a more progressive and equitable world for all.

Shikha Goel, IPS
Head, Women's Safety Wing, Telangana Police

The Kidnapping of Baby Ishitha

My phone rang. It was Poonam's mother, Rakhi. I was a bit taken aback. Though Poonam was my best friend, her mother and I hardly ever interacted.

'Namaste, aunty! How are you?' I said, trying to hide my surprise.

'I am okay, beta! How are you?'

'Okay, aunty. Tell me, how can I help?'

'It's about Poonam,' she said in a voice shot with anxiety. 'She hasn't been well lately, and I was wondering if you could visit her. She always seems to cheer up when you're around.'

'Sure, aunty. I had been wondering too why she hadn't called me for the past one week, but I was kind of busy with my exams and didn't get time to check on her either.'

Rakhi aunty sighed deeply. 'How I wish I hadn't rushed Poonam into marriage when she was just a schoolgirl,' she lamented, her voice choking with emotion. 'She could have had a life filled with so much more joy if only we had let her pursue her studies. But her father, he was unyielding back then, and you understand how we could never defy his commands... I was a coward, Naina. Had I been stronger, we might've found a way out, somehow.'

Candle in the Wind

'You did what you thought was best for her, aunty.' I said a bit awkwardly.

'Yes, but what we did didn't turn out to be so good for her. She is desperately unhappy, Naina!' There was a hint of a sob in Rakhi aunty's voice.

'What's happened, aunty?' I asked, my concern growing.

'I can't explain over the phone. Please come down to meet her as soon as you can and please call her now. She needs you, Naina; you always had a calming influence on her.'

'Of course, I'd be happy to call her. Is she okay? Can you tell me what's wrong?'

There was a hesitant pause at the other end. Then, Rakhi aunty said, 'It's something that her father is about to do... And I can't stop him as he never listens to me. Poonam is so angry with us that she is refusing to take my calls. She'll explain... You talk to her, please!'

I wondered why Rakhi aunty couldn't explain the problem over the phone. But I didn't want to push her because she was clearly uncomfortable talking about it.

'Sure, aunty. I'll call her immediately. Don't worry. Everything will be fine.'

'Thank you so much, Naina. I know you are a good friend to her and you might be able to help. Why don't you come down and meet her? That might be better.'

'I wish I could, aunty,' I said regretfully. 'But I have my final exams next week...' There was a reproachful silence at the other end. I felt guilty, and quickly added, 'I'll call her right now. And after my exams, I'll come and spend the day with her. Hopefully, she'll feel comfortable enough to share what's on her mind.'

This seemed to satisfy Rakhi aunty. She thanked me once more and hung up.

I called Poonam. She answered in a listless voice.

'Hi, how are you?' I asked brightly.

'I'm fine,' she said.

She certainly didn't sound fine.

'C'mon, you can tell me. What's really going on? Your mom is so worried that she called me, and I can make out from your voice something's bothering you.'

'Nothing re! I'm fine. How are you?'

'Not well. Final exams will start in two days. Look, I'll come down and visit you as soon as my exams are over. How about that?'

'That'll be great!' Poonam sounded happier.

'Great, my last exam is on next Friday and I'll come on Saturday.'

'Sure, I look forward to your visit,' Poonam said. From her voice I could feel her smiling.

The day after my exams, I boarded a bus to Khasampur. This small village—in Bidar, Karnataka—holds a special place in my heart. I spent many happy years of my childhood there, and that is when Poonam and I became best friends. But fate took us in different directions. Circumstances led my family to move to Kamthana, a neighbouring town near the Telangana-Karnataka border, when I was twelve years old, while Poonam remained in Khasampur, and was now married.

I remembered my school days. The children would never include me when they played hide-and-seek or other games.

'You are a *kuntivadu*, a cripple! How can you run?' They would tell me. Some even chanted 'Kuntivadu! Kuntivadu!' I pretended I couldn't care less. I pretended I'd rather read than play their silly games.

I was a sickly child, prone to epileptic fits. As if that was not enough, I also had a limp due to polio. My mother, Tara, had taken me to various doctors, hoping for a cure, but the limp persisted. I was often the target of ridicule of the other girls in school.

I would sit in the classroom and eat lunch alone, pretending to read a book I had borrowed from the library. Most of my classmates borrowed books only because they were forced to read. But I loved our library. Though I studied in a small school, it had a large shelf of story books. I could escape into the world of stories, into a fairy-tale world where everybody was kind and good always prevailed over evil.

Initially, I wasn't very close to Poonam. I had no friends, while Poonam had plenty. I liked her too, because she never teased me about my limp and was always polite and friendly.

What made my school days bearable were my teachers. I was good at studies and they encouraged me. I was the girl who always topped the class, and they applauded my efforts. But they never made me the class leader. Perhaps they understood that none of the other children would listen to me.

One day, the maths teacher admonished Poonam for not doing her homework. 'Complete the homework during lunch and hand it over to me before you leave school,' he told her.

So, Poonam didn't go with the other children during lunch. She sat crying in class, trying to complete the maths homework, while I kept glancing at her covertly. Clearly, she was struggling to solve the problems.

Finally, I asked shyly, 'Can I help you?'

She nodded gratefully. 'Will you?'

I solved the problems in a rough notebook, which Poonam then copied in her class notebook. After that, she became friendlier and even protected me from the bullies. I, in turn, helped her with her studies as she was not a very bright student. Soon we became close. Children can be cruel, but Poonam was a warm and compassionate soul who never laughed at my shortcomings. We began to study together and she became more interested in studies as she understood the concepts better. She never topped the class, but she did become an above-average student. Though she was Hindu and I was Christian, we had no problems overcoming our religious differences and became unconditional friends for life.

When my family moved out of the village in search of better prospects, I was sad to leave. Poonam and I promised to always keep in touch. And, over the years, we managed to stay in touch and even meet in person when Poonam came to visit her mother's family in Kamthana.

On the bus to Khasampur, I reflected on our friendship

that had stood the test of time and distance.

My life and Poonam's were as different as day and night. My parents focused on my education and future career, even though they barely had enough money to make ends meet. Somebody informed them about the disability benefits provided by the government and my education became almost free.

Poonam's life took a different turn. I still remember the day she called me up and sobbed into the phone.

'What happened, Poonam?' I asked.

'My parents don't want me to go to school anymore,' she cried.

'But why?'

'Nanna says he has found a good match for me in the village. The boy's parents are not asking for a very hefty dowry, as this is his second marriage. His first wife passed away recently. Nanna doesn't want to let this opportunity pass.'

'And are you okay with this?' I asked, concerned.

'My opinion doesn't count! My mother protested but he wouldn't listen to her either. They had a fight and he beat her and threatened to turn her out of the house. After that, my mother didn't dare to protest anymore,' Poonam said bitterly.

'Why are they marrying you off so early? Don't they want you to get educated?' I asked in surprise.

'Nanna says that for the last two years the harvest has not been good. It seems he has lots of debts and can't afford to send all of us to school anymore.' She let out a tiny little sob.

I felt my heart would break. Poonam had two more sisters and a brother who was only in nursery.

Despite her objections, Poonam was married off. I attended the wedding. I had never seen a gloomier bride. The groom was a balding man, at least twenty years older than her. I felt bad for my friend. In a way, I was thankful that my parents had more modern views about how a girl child should be treated.

As for me, I pursued my studies with the dream of building a career as a teacher for differently-abled children. My own experience of being treated differently because of my limp fuelled my passion for caring for differently-abled children. I completed my higher secondary education with good marks and got admission into Carmel D.Ed. College, after which I planned to pursue my dream of working in a school for the differently-abled.

∞

The bus halted at the Khasampur bus stop. As I stepped out into the familiar surroundings of the village, memories flooded my mind. The parched earth emitted its distinct aroma, mingled with the sweet fragrance of mango blossoms and the smoke from cow-dung fires, instantly transporting me back to my childhood days. I started to walk towards Poonam's home, still lost in childhood memories. Suddenly, my foot hit a small stone and I nearly fell, my shorter left foot hampering my balance. The jolt brought me back to the present and I noticed that I had nearly reached

Poonam's home. But there was no sign of her. Instead, I saw her mother-in-law, Kavitha, a rather intimidating woman, sitting on the porch. Kavitha brusquely informed me that Poonam was at a health camp in the field where the annual fair was being held.

I hurried towards the field. As I entered the fair, the vibrant atmosphere filled me with excitement. The colourful stalls, the aroma of freshly cooked snacks, and the laughter of children playing games added to the festive spirit. I spotted the health camp in one corner of the field.

I entered the tent, hoping to find Poonam. I spotted her lying on a charpoy, looking frail and weak. My heart skipped a beat as I walked towards her. It had been so long since we had seen each other; the sight of her in such a condition left me deeply concerned. She was engaged in an intense conversation with a volunteer nurse and didn't notice me approaching.

'I really want to have a child, but I don't know why it's not happening,' she was saying plaintively to the nurse. 'My husband and mother-in-law are so angry with me. Please, please help me. Please give me some medicine.'

The nurse was sympathetic. 'I understand your desire, but our health camp is limited in resources. Unfortunately, we can't provide the medical treatment you need here. You need to visit a proper hospital in the city. They have better facilities and specialists who can help you with your condition.'

Poonam looked up and saw me. Her face lit up for a moment, but then her expression changed and she fell silent,

The Kidnapping of Baby Ishitha

looking troubled. Obviously, she hadn't wanted me to know.

'Poonam, why didn't you tell me you were unwell? I'm your friend, no?' I asked, running my hand over her head gently.

Poonam said nothing. Tears rolled down the corner of her eyes as she squeezed my hand.

The nurse said gently, 'You need to get up now. Other patients are waiting.'

We walked back slowly to Poonam's home. I held her hand, trying to offer whatever comfort I could. 'Poonam,' I said softly, 'I'm here for you and we'll find a way to help you, I promise.' She looked at me with tears in her eyes.

'Why were you in the health camp? What's wrong? Why have you become so thin?' Questions tumbled out of my mouth as we walked down the narrow mud roads through the fields, back to her home.

Poonam sat down abruptly under a tree and started weeping.

'What happened? Don't cry, please,' I pleaded, tenderly wiping her face, my own heart heavy with pain.

'I am unable to bear a child. My in-laws are harassing me so much. They are telling me that they will arrange for another marriage for my husband. They have approached my parents, asking for my sister's hand for him!'

'This is shocking! And your parents are agreeable to this arrangement?'

'My mother protested. But my father never listens to her. Naina, you know my parents are not well off. I have three more sisters. Meena, my younger sister, is also reaching marriageable age. They can marry off two of us with minimal cost. So yes, my father agreed, and my mother's wish or my wish never mattered anyway. I wish I were dead!'

'Oh my god! And what about your husband?'

'He says he will have to abide by his amma's wishes. My mother-in-law is a *mantragatte*, a witch. Within six months of our marriage, she started to pressure me for a child. I hate her! And I hate my husband as well. He is such a weak character. Always eager to please his parents at all costs,' Poonam said, blowing her nose into the pallu of her sari.

'How do you know that it's not a problem with your husband?' I asked.

'My husband says that he checked with a doctor.'

'He's lying. He would need to take you along for the check-up,' I said grimly. 'I have read these things as a part of my graduation training.'

'His elder brother has lots of kids. So I don't think the problem is with him, Naina.' Poonam wiped away her tears and tried to compose herself. '*Ee panikirani charchalu inka apudam*, let's skip this useless discussion! I'm so happy that you travelled all this way just to see me. You are a true friend!' Her voice was choked with emotion.

'I was missing you, re! That's why I came down.' I said, hugging her.

'You are lucky. Your parents allowed you to study, you are going to college, and soon you'll get a job. My parents never bothered with my education.'

I felt embarrassed and even a little guilty about my own good fortune. There was an awkward pause as I searched

The Kidnapping of Baby Ishitha

for a suitable response. Without waiting for my response, Poonam got to her feet. 'Come, let's go. My mother-in-law will get upset if I don't get back home soon. Stay back for lunch!'

When we reached her house, Kavitha was still sitting on the porch of the small house, methodically cleaning and chopping up spinach. A small baby was sleeping peacefully on a folded sari on the floor next to her. A tiny mosquito net was placed over the baby. Two young boys, aged approximately four or five, were engrossed in a Telugu cartoon show on a small TV in the drawing room, which was visible from the porch too.

Poonam introduced me to Kavitha, who didn't bother to dredge up a smile. 'There is rice boiling on the fire. Check on it. And start peeling some garlic. I can't do all the work!' She snapped at Poonam, completely ignoring me. Poonam nodded and obediently walked towards the kitchen. I followed her. The kitchen was in a secluded corner of the porch. The aroma of boiling rice wafted in the air.

From the kitchen, I could see another room. The door was open, and I could see a woman, probably the mother of the small baby, lying on a bed, talking on her mobile.

'Who is she?' I asked Poonam in a whisper.

'My bhabi. My husband's elder brother's wife,' Poonam whispered back.

'Why is she not helping you?' I asked in an indignant voice.

'She is my mother-in-law's favourite. She has three kids, all boys. My mother-in-law treats her like a queen.'

'And she treats you like an unpaid maid.' I commented grimly. 'I had better go. I don't think she'll like it if I stay for lunch.'

Poonam nodded sadly in agreement. 'Yes…I think you should.'

Six months later, I received the news of Poonam's death. Immediately, I rushed to the village. Poonam's body lay on the porch of her parents' home, decked with flowers. Clearly, since our last meeting she had thinned down even further, reduced to a shadow of her former self.

'*Aharanni jirnincukoleka anarogyaniki gurayyadu. Maranincadu*, she was sick, couldn't digest her food, and hence she died,' said her mother as she wept.

I saw her husband, Ravi, standing at a distance, quiet and sombre.

I got the complete story from a common friend, Savitri. Even a year after her marriage, Poonam had not conceived. The taunts started, and after my visit, Ravi married her younger sister. For Poonam's parents, it was a win-win situation—both daughters married at the cost of one. Poonam was shunted off to her parents' home.

Within a month of her sister's marriage, the news of an impending childbirth reached Poonam. That was when the first signs of depression became noticeable. She stopped taking my calls. But I wasn't able to follow up on her either, as I had completed my D.Ed. and got a job looking after differently-abled children. I had been too busy to take care of my friend. Savitri told me that Poonam would often weep, throw temper tantrums and develop a low-degree fever. For those around her, this meant she had gone mad. No efforts were made to get her treated. Her health wasn't a priority for anybody, except perhaps for her poor mother. But her mother had no money for treatment. Within four months, Poonam was dead.

I was consumed with guilt and grief. I felt I had betrayed my friend. At the same time, I shuddered at Poonam's fate and wondered what would happen if I got married and couldn't bear children.

∽

A year had passed since Poonam died. I was working at the Rainbow Special School, a Christian missionary school that catered to differently-abled children in Kamthana. I was earning a decent salary of ₹25,000 per month.

My parents started looking for a groom for me, but nobody who matched my education or my income levels showed much interest. I couldn't really blame them. Who would wish to marry a thin, dark, unattractive girl like me? Especially a girl who had a limp and was epileptic. I was almost resigned to the fact that nobody would ever marry me. To my surprise, however, a family from Bidar expressed interest in an alliance. Their son's name was Anil Joseph. After initial rounds of talks among the elders, they wanted to see me in person.

My would-be groom had not completed tenth standard. He ran a small grocery store and was shorter than me. Still, my parents convinced me to meet him. 'Please, Naina.

Despite knowing that you had polio and have a limp, they want to go ahead with the alliance. There's no harm talking to them once. You can see that there is nobody else who is even remotely interested.'

'Probably, the fact that I work in Rainbow School and earn a decent salary made them interested in me,' I told my parents cynically.

So, I was decked up for the occasion. The cozy living room of our modest home buzzed with anticipation as we awaited the arrival of our guests. I stayed in the bedroom that I shared with my sister. I had left the bedroom door slightly ajar, so that I could peep into the drawing room, and had switched off the bedroom light so that it would be difficult to see inside. Outside, my parents and my younger brother and sister waited for the possible groom and his family, their faces a picture of hope and anxiety.

The doorbell rang and my father rushed to welcome our guests. I peered out cautiously and saw Mr and Mrs Joseph, a middle-aged couple dressed in traditional Indian attire, enter our home. Their son, Anil, stood beside them, his nervousness palpable.

'Please come in. We're delighted to have you here,' my father said with a welcoming smile.

'Thank you for inviting us, Mr Fernandes,' Mrs Joseph replied graciously.

My mother rose and said, 'I'll get some tea for you.' She silently gestured to my sister and together they went to the kitchen.

My sister came to our bedroom. 'Didi, come. Amma

wants you to carry the tea tray in,' she whispered.

I walked into the drawing room with a tray of tea and snacks, making an effort to hide my limp as much as I could. Anil and his parents greeted me with smiles, their curiosity evident in their expressions.

Anil gave me a faint, embarrassed smile while his parents greeted me with a warm 'hello'.

As we settled down with our tea and snacks, the conversation began.

'So, Anil, tell us a bit about yourself,' my father eased into the conversation.

Anil looked slightly uncomfortable as he replied, 'Well, I run a small grocery store nearby. I stopped studying after completing my ninth standard and have been working ever since.'

Mr Joseph chimed in, 'Our Anil was never good at studies. But he has a sharp mind and is handling his business extremely well.'

My mother spoke up. 'Naina has completed her graduation. She's a teacher at a school for differently-abled children.'

Anil seemed impressed. 'Education is very essential.'

I smiled, sensing a connection through our shared appreciation for knowledge and learning.

As the conversation continued, my father subtly broached the topic of my epilepsy.

'Anil, there's something important you should know about Naina. We had mentioned this before to Ramesh, but I don't know if he informed you clearly. Naina sometimes gets epileptic fits.' Ramesh was our neighbour who had connected the Josephs with us.

Tension suddenly filled the room, and the Josephs exchanged worried glances.

'Epilepsy? Since when?' Mrs Joseph asked with concern.

My father responded calmly, 'She has had it since childhood, but it's well-managed with medication. She rarely has seizures now.'

Mrs Joseph appeared hesitant. 'I see... We weren't aware of this.'

A heavy silence settled over the room, and my parents looked visibly apprehensive.

My mother said, 'We wanted to be honest and open about everything. It's crucial that both families are comfortable with this match.'

Mr Joseph sighed, his conflict evident. 'We need some time to think about it.'

After this, the conversation became stilted and awkward, and soon my parents escorted the Josephs to the door, leaving me alone in the living room with my siblings.

'They have rejected you,' my rather insensitive sister told me. 'They ran away as soon as they heard you have epilepsy.'

'Good riddance, I say,' my brother consoled me. 'I didn't like the look of the boy at all.'

I took a deep breath, trying not to cry. But I remained positive. Though this match may not have worked out, I remained hopeful that one day I would find someone who appreciated me for the person that I was inside.

There were more potential suitors after Anil, but all of them rejected me as soon as they came to know of my epilepsy. My parents had allowed me to save the money that I earned. My father advised me to keep the money in a fixed deposit in my name, which I did.

'Don't worry, Naina. Marriage is not everything in life,' he would tell me. 'Save the money and invest wisely. Why do you need a man in your life? You are a strong and independent young woman who is beautiful on the inside. You are our little princess.'

But I wanted to get married. I saw many of my friends getting married, having kids and forming loving relationships with their husbands, and I felt sad and envious. Yes, I had seen Poonam too. She had suffered. But I was sure that I would have a better life than hers. After all, I was more qualified.

I was only human and craved for what was out of reach. I was financially independent, educated, and had a stable job that I loved. Yet, I wasn't happy. I wanted a husband and a child, a family of my own.

In January 2018, three years after I started working, my parents were finally able to find a match for me. All they could manage was an illiterate fruit vendor from Hyderabad. After so many rejections, we had decided not to tell my husband's family that I suffered from epilepsy.

I quit my job and moved to LB Nagar, Hyderabad, where my husband Seemon resided with his parents.

My mother-in-law, Estel, was a bossy and nosy woman, but I managed to remain in her good books by taking over all the household work from her. I hadn't learned how to cook before my marriage. Estel taught me, and I was a model student. I was a little sad that my husband was illiterate while I came from a well-educated family. But he was a good, mild-mannered man, and I adjusted. My new family was open to the idea of me getting a job, and I started applying for suitable positions. But getting a job in my limited field of specialization wasn't easy.

Six months into the marriage, I had my first fight with my mother-in-law. I was busy making breakfast in the kitchen and the delicious smell of sambar and idli filled the tiny apartment. Estel had a headache and she rummaged through my cupboard for tablets without my permission. That was when she discovered the contraceptives. A devout Catholic, Estel was devastated.

'Naina!' She thundered, marching into the kitchen. 'What are these pills?'

I looked at the incriminating bottle in her hand. 'It's... it's...' I stammered.

'It's a contraceptive pill. Isn't it? Now don't try to lie to me!'

I nodded dumbly. I wanted to avoid getting pregnant until I got a job. But I couldn't tell this to Estel as she was a devout Catholic.

Lowering her voice, she said, 'I am throwing these away. Don't dare to use such pills again. You know contraceptives are against our religion! Does Seemon know that you are using contraceptive pills?'

I shook my head.

'I thought so,' Estel said grimly. 'You are hiding your

activities from everybody! I want a grandchild soon. Do you understand? I will talk to Seemon once he comes home.'

Estel complained to Seemon as soon as he returned from work. Seemon scolded me and forbade me from using contraceptives.

I had always been proud of my education and financial independence, but it now struck me like a blow that my situation was no different from Poonam's. However, after a while, I shrugged off my misgivings. With my limp and unattractive looks, I couldn't get a better husband. I would have to be happy with whatever husband God had given me.

Everybody was thrilled when I became pregnant. As a reward, my in-laws allowed me to go out on a movie and dinner date with my husband. However, the happiness was short-lived. In my eighth month, I suddenly got an epileptic fit and fell down. The fall caused me to suffer a miscarriage.

Estel was livid. 'I don't know what kind of woman I've got my son married to. Why didn't you inform us that you have epilepsy?'

'I didn't have epilepsy before marriage. This is the first time I had an epileptic fit.' I lied desperately.

'You're lying,' Estel said flatly. She called up my mother and cursed her for hiding the fact that I was epileptic. I felt bad for my mother but did not dare to stand up for her.

Seemon was also upset with me. This time he beat me, while Estel looked on.

'Why didn't you tell us about your epilepsy? How could you and your family cheat us in this manner? I want a baby at all costs. Otherwise, I'll take a new wife.'

My world came crashing down around me. I remembered Poonam. How that girl must have suffered, I thought with a sense of déjà vu. It was as if Poonam's story was repeating itself. Only this time, I was the victim.

I cried and cried. Soon, Seemon took pity on me and tried to console me. He had come to love me. We made up. His parents, however, were not so easily appeased.

I was young and resilient. Within a few weeks, I became pregnant again. This time I was determined to carry the baby to term at all costs. I started going to church regularly and prayed fervently.

But bad things happen all the time to good people who've done nothing to deserve them. In my fourth month, I began to bleed heavily. I hid it from my family and secretly visited a doctor. The doctor confirmed my worst fears—I had miscarried once again.

I stood at the bus stand near the hospital, waiting for the bus home. But when it came, I couldn't board it. Moving behind a pillar for a modicum of privacy, I let silent tears flow from my eyes, oblivious to the pitying glances of passers-by.

Finally, one elderly woman asked in a tender voice, 'Amma, why are you crying? Is there some way I can help?'

I looked up and realized that I was attracting attention and pity from the bystanders. I quickly wiped my eyes and shook my head to indicate that I didn't need any help. I left the bus stop in a hurry and started walking back home. Walking would help me think, I thought feverishly. I couldn't allow my husband to remarry. I could not allow my life to end up like Poonam's.

The Kidnapping of Baby Ishitha

When I reached home, I still had no clue how to salvage the situation. All I knew was that I couldn't let my husband or in-laws know about my miscarriage.

I pretended I was still pregnant. I stuffed some clothes under my salwar-kameez to simulate a pregnant belly and faked morning sickness and fatigue. Finally, the eighth month of my pregnancy arrived. Hesitantly, I told my husband that I wanted to go to my parents' for childbirth. Seemon agreed happily, relieved that my parents would bear the cost of childbirth.

Seemon and I boarded a bus for Kamthana, Bidar, from MG Bus Station. I could finally relax a bit. I had spent the past four months in extreme tension, always worried that Estel or Seemon would come to know that I was faking my pregnancy.

Seemon returned home after spending two happy days in Bidar, where my parents treated him like royalty.

But my mother, Tara, was worried that my stomach did not look big enough for a nine-month pregnancy. 'Let's get a check up with a doctor, Naina,' she said. 'I don't want you to give birth to a stillborn child. Your stomach should have grown a lot more.'

'Don't worry, amma, I'm fine,' I tried to appease her.

'Please, Naina, you know the consequences if something happens to the baby,' my mother pleaded.

'Yes, I know. I know what a great family you have married me into,' I snapped irritably.

Visiting a doctor would expose my fake pregnancy. Tension was building up in me; I was spending sleepless nights trying to devise ways of procuring a baby.

Finally, unable to bear my mother's nagging, I agreed to visit the doctor in the Bidar Maternity Hospital. When we went, there was a huge crowd. 'Abba! Why so much crowd?' I asked a nearby patient who was waiting in queue with us.

'Mondays are always busy days in any hospital. Mostly, doctors are not available on weekends. So there's more of a rush on Mondays,' the patient explained.

As we waited, my heart thudded furiously as I tried to think of a way out of my predicament.

After three hours, we were finally called by the doctor for consultation. 'I'll talk to the doctor alone. I cannot speak freely in front of you,' I snapped at my mother, marvelling at my acting ability.

Thinking that her usually mild-mannered and composed daughter was being unreasonable due to her pregnant condition, my mother agreed to stay outside.

Inside the doctor's chamber, the doctor examined me.

'You aren't pregnant! What's this? Why are you wasting my time?' The doctor asked me in surprise and anger.

'Please, doctor, don't inform my family!' I begged, folding my hands in front of her, tears falling from my eyes. 'They think I am eight-and-a-half months pregnant.'

'Why are you doing this?' She asked.

I explained my situation to her.

'But how long can you fool them?' The doctor asked compassionately.

'I'll find some way,' I replied.

The doctor, who was overworked and underpaid, shrugged and let me go.

As I walked out, I pasted a smile on my face. 'Everything's fine,' I told my mother.

During the long wait in the queue, I had formulated a plan for procuring a baby. I began to set it in place now.

'The doctor said I should check into a bigger hospital just to be on the safe side.'

'Oh! So what can we do?' My mother asked, flustered.

'I'll go to the government hospital in Sultan Bazar, Hyderabad. They have excellent doctors there.'

'How can you go alone? I'll come with you!' My mother objected.

'Then who'll look after the rest of the family? No, no, amma. I'll go on my own. Seemon is there to help me. Stop worrying!'

'Your father won't allow you to go on your own,' my mother said.

'Please, amma… *Please* convince him. Let me sort this out on my own. Please, amma…'

My mother reluctantly agreed.

The next day, I packed a couple of sarees in a bag and set out for Hyderabad. On the way, I withdrew part of my savings from an ATM. I was grateful to my father for his sound advice on saving my money. The money would come in handy now for what I was about to do. As I waited at the bus station to board a bus for Hyderabad, I noticed someone had forgotten a plastic bag in a corner. I looked around but found no one who seemed interested in the plastic bag. I picked up the bag with the intent of depositing it at the lost-and-found counter. When I looked in, I found it had a saree and a purse with an Aadhaar card in it. Suddenly, I had an idea. I could use the Aadhaar card. I knew that one needed to show ID proof when checking into a hotel. I deposited the bag at the lost-and-found counter as planned, but kept the Aadhaar card.

On 29 June 2018, I arrived at the MG Bus Station in Hyderabad. The sky was overcast, and there were intermittent showers. I checked into a busy lodge, close to the bus stop, using the Aadhaar card I had found. After checking in, I walked the two kilometres from MG Road to the maternity hospital in Sultan Bazar. I had deliberately taken accommodation quite far away from the hospital so that if the police got involved and checked the nearby lodges, they would not be able to trace me.

I entered the hospital to recce the area. I noted that the nurses were wearing blue sarees or salwar suits. I loitered around for some time, checking out the outpatient departments and then the maternity ward. The latter was a long, spacious hall with at least fifty beds. The mothers were sleeping or chatting with other patients and relatives, their newborn babies lying close to them. Several nurses were moving around, tending to the patients. Some were taking the babies from the mothers to the next ward where they were being vaccinated. The wailing babies were then brought back to their mothers, who soothed them and rocked them to sleep. As I watched the babies with their mothers, my resolve wavered. I gazed at the innocent lives before me, their vulnerability tugging at my conscience. Tears welled up in my eyes and doubt clawed at my determination. My conscience whispered to me, 'You can't do this. It's wrong.' But the thought of my in-laws' anger and the possibility of losing Seemon flooded back into my mind. My desperation returned. I studied the scene, managing to blend into the background. Then, without attracting attention, I walked out of the hospital.

The next day, I was back again at a different time. I repeated this for several days, trying to determine the best time to snatch a baby without attracting attention.

Each time my conscience resurfaced, warning me that my impending actions were morally wrong, I stifled it ruthlessly. I was filled with cold determination. My marriage was at stake here. I knew I wouldn't have a place in my marital home if I returned without a child.

I called my mother that evening and fabricated a lie. 'The doctor mentioned some complications with my pregnancy, so I have been hospitalized. She even mentioned the possibility that the baby may be born premature.'

My mother got flustered. 'Should I come down? But then, it will be so difficult for the entire family if I go to Hyderabad. Your brother Jacob won't be able to come as his MCom exams are going on. Why don't I send Genelia?'

Genelia was my sister, and the two of us didn't get along. I said, 'Don't fuss, amma. I don't want Genelia around. This is a difficult time for me. Don't add to my difficulties. You know she's a silly girl and won't be able to help me at all. Anyway, Seemon is here with me. We'll manage. Don't worry about me. I'll call you again soon.'

Meanwhile, monsoon had started in earnest. The rainfall, which had been scanty so far, was making up for the lapse. I had now taken a room in a cheap lodge just outside the hospital. I went there only to sleep at night, carefully covering my face with the pallu of my saree so that nobody could get a good glimpse of my face. The rest of the day, I loitered inside and outside the hospital, carefully recceing the scene. I knew that I would have to kidnap a baby soon; I was a sickly person and would fall seriously ill if I continued to get drenched every day.

On 1 July, a Sunday, I went to church and prayed for the success of my plan. I knew I was about to commit a crime, and if I was caught, not only would I land up in jail, but my husband would also throw me out of his life. Standing alone in the quiet church, I folded my hands in prayer, my voice quivering as I spoke to God.

> *I know I've never been the most devout of your children, but today, I come before you in desperate need of guidance, forgiveness and strength. You see, I've reached a point in my life where I'm trapped in a whirlwind of deceit and despair, and I don't know whom else to turn to.*
>
> *Dear God, you know my story. You know how much I have suffered. I'm terrified, God. Terrified of losing the man I love, terrified of being abandoned because I can't give him the child he so desperately desires. And in my desperation, I've made this plan to steal a baby from the maternity hospital, an innocent child who deserves a*

loving family and a chance at a happy life. It's a crime I cannot even fathom committing, but I fear it may be the only way to save my marriage; the only way to prevent it from crumbling.

I know what I am about to do is wrong, God. I know it's a sin beyond measure. But in this moment of despair, I beg for your forgiveness, your guidance, and your strength to carry this burden. Help me find a way out of this darkness, a way to save my marriage without causing harm to another innocent soul. I am lost, God, but I pray that you can help me find a path back to light, to redemption, and to a love based on truth and honesty. Please show me the way, for I am a desperate soul in need of your mercy.

Amen.

∞

The previous day, I had gone to a nearby shop and bought a blue saree that was a close match to the kind of sarees I had seen the nurses wearing. I called my mother and told her that my pregnancy was proceeding well and the doctor would deliver the baby in a day or two.

I had decided that I would try to kidnap a baby around 10.00 a.m. the next day, a Monday. As I had learned, Mondays were the busiest days in any hospital. Around 10.00 a.m., the nurses would be busy vaccinating the babies and taking care of the mothers. There would be lots of visitors, and the ward would be crowded. I decided to abandon my bag in which I had packed my sarees. I also left the stolen Aadhaar card behind. I was careful to put my own Aadhaar and ATM cards in plastic covers and tucked them into my blouse. Wearing my new blue saree, I walked into the hospital. My heart was racing though I tried to keep a poker face. As I had anticipated, the maternity ward was crowded.

I approached a patient closest to the exit.

'Hand over the baby. It needs to be vaccinated,' I told the mother in a voice as brisk as I could make it. The mother had been chatting with a man sitting next to her who appeared to be her husband.

'Who are you?' The husband asked in a hostile voice.

'I am a nurse here. The baby needs vaccination.'

'The baby was vaccinated yesterday. Don't you know?' The husband asked, his tone growing increasingly suspicious.

I backtracked quickly.

'Oh, is it? There must be a mistake in the paperwork! I'll go and check with the doctor.'

I hurried out of the maternity ward, my heart racing. I had nearly been caught! I went to a nearby toilet and washed my face, trying to calm myself. I had been taking very little food for the past few days and felt dizzy and disoriented. However, the water I splashed on my face revived me.

I realized I had made a mistake approaching a woman who had an attendant with her. After composing myself, I walked back to the maternity ward again, trying to find a woman who was unattended. As I was scanning the hall desperately, I saw a man at a nearby bed get up from his

The Kidnapping of Baby Ishitha

seat and tell his wife, 'I'll go down and pay the bills. I'll be back soon.'

I followed the man to see where he was going. He went out of the hospital, and I guessed that he had gone for some tea. Assured that he wouldn't be back for at least half an hour, I rushed back to the maternity ward. The woman was feeling drowsy. The baby lying next to her started to cry. I waited as she fed her baby, and both mother and baby fell asleep. Then, I walked purposefully to the bed and nudged the woman. 'Madam, wake up!' I said in a brusque voice, like that of the nurses I had observed for the last few days. The woman woke up with a jerk.

'I need to take the baby for vaccination,' I said in an authoritative tone.

The woman nodded, still in an exhausted state.

I took the baby in my arms. 'Where's the file?' I asked the woman. As she stared at me uncomprehendingly, I repeated in an irritated tone, 'The file, madam?! The papers which have the prescription and other details? Come on, amma! I don't have all day. There are so many patients!'

The woman handed over the file containing the details to me. I pretended to study the file. I saw that it was a baby girl. I wished that the baby had been a boy, but it couldn't be helped. I noted that the mother's name was written as Vijaya.

As I juggled the file with one hand, the baby woke up and started to cry.

'Careful,' Vijaya told me.

'Yes, yes. Don't worry. I'll bring her back in ten minutes,' I assured Vijaya. Somehow, I kept my voice brisk, though I was trembling inside.

Taking the baby and the file, I walked out. The baby started to cry harder as I walked away from the maternity ward. I tried to calm her down as I rapidly walked out of the hospital, careful not to run. It would attract unnecessary attention. At the exit, the guard looked at me suspiciously.

'Why are you taking out a baby, amma?' He asked, looking at the crying baby.

I showed him the file and said, 'This is my baby. I had brought her to the hospital for vaccination.'

The guard let me go. I immediately walked away and took an auto from the nearby auto stand. There was no time to lose. At any moment, the parents might realize that their baby had been kidnapped and rush out and stop me. I asked the auto driver to take me to the MG Bus Station. After paying off the auto, I went into the bus station and bought a ticket for Bidar. The baby was crying continuously. I was at my wits' end. I had no idea how to calm the baby. Was the baby ill? I desperately hoped there was nothing wrong with it.

A tea seller was watching me as I tried to shush the baby. 'Give the baby some milk, amma,' she advised. 'It's obviously hungry. Why didn't you get its milk bottle?'

'Oh, I lost the bag containing the bottles in an auto while coming back from the hospital,' I lied glibly.

'Then go and buy some more. I'll give you some hot water to prepare the milk. There is a medicine shop right

The Kidnapping of Baby Ishitha

outside,' the tea seller said kindly.

I rushed to the nearby medicine shop and bought a milk bottle and Lactogen for the baby. I came back to the tea shop and, taking warm water from the tea seller, I prepared the milk and fed the baby. Thankfully the baby stopped crying and fell asleep after drinking the milk. I prepared one more bottle before getting on the bus for Bidar, which had arrived at the station by that time.

I boarded the bus exultantly. I had not been caught. My racing heart was finally calming down. I looked at the baby. In that sacred moment, I understood that my purpose in life had forever changed. I was a mother now and my heart swelled with a love so pure and fierce that I knew it would guide me through the challenges and joys of parenthood. My baby had filled a void in my soul that I never knew existed, and I embraced this new role with all the love and devotion in my being. And, as I continued to hold my newborn close, I made one final promise to myself: 'No matter what challenges lie ahead, no matter the storms we may face, I will always, *always* love, cherish and protect you, my precious child. You are my heart, my soul, and my greatest blessing.' I decided to name my baby Ishitha, the 'desired one'.

As the bus departed from Hyderabad, a wave of relaxation washed over me, prompting me to doze off. Before long, I found myself immersed in a dream where Vijaya was lamenting, her anguish palpable as she beat her chest. I jerked awake, startling Ishitha, who started crying. Hastily, I retrieved the milk bottle and fed her, and soon she drifted

Candle in the Wind

back into slumber. I felt guilty about taking Ishitha away from Vijaya, but consoled myself. Vijaya could easily bear another child, couldn't she? But where would I get another family if my husband divorced me? I still remembered the frustration I had felt when so many prospective grooms, men with lesser capabilities, rejected me before my marriage to Seemon was finalized.

∞

Back at the Government Maternity Hospital in Sultan Bazar, Vijaya had fallen asleep after handing the baby over to Naina. She had given birth only three days back. It was her first child. She had seen her husband's face turn gloomy when he was told that she had given birth to a girl child. Her heart had sunk to the floor. But her husband had magnanimously taken the baby in his arms. Her own heart had melted when she had seen her child and cradled her in her arms.

But the baby was cranky at night and she had been so weary. When she handed over her baby to the nurse, she knew that she should be alert. But her tired body refused to cooperate with her mind, and she had fallen into a deep sleep.

Meanwhile, Vijaya's husband, Nari, came back to find that Vijaya was sleeping. There was no sign of the baby.

'Where is the baby?' He asked, shaking Vijaya awake.

She woke up with a start. Then she recalled the nurse.

'The nurse had taken the baby for vaccination,' she stammered, her eyes red from lack of sleep.

The Kidnapping of Baby Ishitha

'Which nurse?'

Vijaya looked around drowsily, trying to identify the nurse. She shook her head, 'I can't see her.'

'Well, I guess the nurse will bring her back soon. You go back to sleep. I'll take care of this,' Nari said in a gentle voice. He knew that Vijaya had had a difficult delivery and that the baby had kept her awake most of the night. He felt bad that he had woken her up. He was glad to see Vijaya falling back into sleep almost immediately, oblivious of the world.

He sat down on a chair beside her bed and waited for the nurse to return with the baby. Half an hour passed. The baby had still not been returned. Nari began to feel uncomfortable. Something seemed to be amiss.

A nurse came to a nearby bed to attend to another patient. Nari cleared his throat to attract her attention, and when she glanced in his direction, he asked, 'Madam, some nurse has taken our baby for vaccination and has not brought her back. Do you know what is happening?'

The nurse shrugged. 'I don't know. The vaccines are being given in the next ward. Why don't you go there and enquire?'

Nari went to the next ward. There was no sign of their baby. He asked everybody around, but nobody knew of her. Finally, he realized that their baby had been kidnapped.

He rushed back to his wife and shook her awake again. 'Vijaya, wake up! Our baby is missing. Who took the baby from you?'

The urgency in Nari's voice jolted Vijaya awake. 'Wha-what happened?'

'The baby is not in the hospital. Who took the baby from you?' Nari was getting increasingly agitated.

Vijaya struggled to a sitting position. 'A woman who was wearing a blue saree just like these nurses. She walked with a slight limp.'

'Will you be able to recognize her? Can you identify which of the nurses here took the baby?'

By noon, the entire ward knew from Vijaya's wailing that her baby had been kidnapped. When questioned, the nurses said that there was no nurse in the ward who walked with a limp.

A senior doctor came to Vijaya's bed. 'Go and put in a written complaint to the police. Our hospital falls under the jurisdiction of the Sultan Bazar Police Station. Crying won't help,' she urged, not unkindly.

Nari rushed to the Sultan Bazar Police Station. The constable who met him took down his written complaint immediately. He was very sympathetic when he realized Nari's plight.

'Wait, I'll see if we can register an FIR immediately. I'll speak to Inspector Naresh and see what we can do.'

The kidnapping of a baby was a serious offence and it was treated as such by the Telangana Police. When SI Naresh Kumar came to know about the kidnapping, he immediately registered an FIR and swung into action. He consulted the head of the Sultan Bazar Police Station, Inspector Shiv Shankar Rao, who informed his higher-ups. The Additional Commissioner of Police, Crimes & SIT, was put in charge of the case by the Commissioner of Police, who emphasized that this was a serious case and that she should leave no stone unturned to solve it. He would help her in any way he could.

Under the ACP's guidance, the police swung into action. Additional Inspector Vamsi Kumar, a star performer in the force, was made the Lead Investigation Officer. Three constables were assigned to him to assist with the investigation. The clues team was contacted to assist with the collection of clues, like checking CCTV footage, taking photos of the crime scene, etc. Within five hours of registering the FIR, the police had started their investigation.

Additional Inspector Vamsi Kumar visited the hospital along with officers of the clues team and met the administrative head.

'Mr Sheshadri, I have received a complaint from Mr Nari that his baby girl has been kidnapped from the hospital,' Vamsi Kumar said.

Requesting the inspector to take a seat, Sheshadri asked his PA over the intercom to send Dr Srilakshmi to his office. Putting down the receiver, he said, 'Inspector Vamsi, thanks for coming immediately. I'll ask the head doctor to meet you and take you to the maternity ward. Dear God! This is so bad! That foolish woman just handed over the baby to an unknown woman. How ridiculous! Already our staff is overworked, and on top of that, this new issue!'

'Yes, yes. Don't worry. We are here to help you,' Inspector Vamsi said, trying to calm the irate administrative head. 'Just instruct your security team and also the doctors and nurses to cooperate with us. We'll take care of the rest.'

By this time, Dr Srilakshmi had come to Seshadri's office.

'Ah! Dr Srilakshmi, Inspector Vamsi is here to investigate the kidnapping of the baby. Please cooperate with him in the investigation. Also, please ensure that the nurses cooperate with him.'

Meanwhile, the clues team, consisting of photographers and sketch artists, had already started their work. The photographers were taking photos of the maternity ward and the surrounding areas. The CCTV footage was being inspected with the help of the hospital's CCTV technician. The team found the footage of a woman in a blue saree clutching a baby and hurrying towards the exit, around the same time Vijaya had handed over her daughter to the unknown woman. The footage was shown to Vijaya. In between sobs, she immediately recognized the woman in the blue saree as the one who had pretended to be a nurse and taken her baby.

'Copy this footage to a CD and give it to us,' the clues team instructed the CCTV technician.

They found more footage from a camera at the exit, showing the woman taking an auto from the hospital gate.

'Check if you can get any more CCTV footage from

The Kidnapping of Baby Ishitha

neighbouring areas that captures the auto or the woman. Also, check with the auto drivers if they can recall dropping the woman somewhere,' Vamsi instructed his team members.

Inspector Vamsi and a few others interviewed the guard, Ramachandran, at the main exit point. Ramachandran recalled the woman as soon as he saw the CCTV footage.

'Why didn't you stop her?' Vamsi asked.

'S-she showed me all the papers. She told me it was her b-baby. How could I have stopped her?' The security guard stammered.

'Okay, okay. Is there a security guard at the maternity ward?'

'Ye-ye-yes, sir. There is a lady security guard.'

'Get her. I want to talk to her.'

But the lady security guard, Vinita, hadn't noticed anything unusual.

'Okay, ma,' Vamsi said, controlling his impatience. He knew that patience was crucial in any successful investigation.

He instructed the sketch artist to speak to the hospital administration and make a sketch of the layout of the hospital, highlighting all the entry and exit points.

The team members who had been sent to inspect the CCTV footage from nearby buildings drew a blank. Such was the case also with those who had gone to question the auto drivers.

Inspector Vamsi returned to the police station with the hospital CCTV footage and immediately updated his senior, Inspector Shiv Shankar Rao, about his findings. An urgent meeting was held with senior police officers along with the ACP, Crimes & SIT.

'This is a reprehensible crime,' the ACP said. 'We will circulate this footage as widely as possible. We need the public's help to trace this woman. The media can broadcast the CCTV footage of the woman on TV. We will also put a lookout notice in newspapers with her picture. Also, I have formed teams that will be headed by some of you. I will share the details shortly. These teams will be responsible for searching major bus and railway stations. My gut feeling is that we will be able to locate the woman in a bus or train station. The kidnapping happened around 11.00 a.m. We have footage of the woman taking an auto. Check the CCTV footage of the bus and railway stations between 11.00 a.m. and 3.00 p.m. I am sure we will be able to trace her in one of those places.'

The ACP's gut feeling proved right. The investigators found CCTV footage of the same woman in a blue saree limping into the MG Bus Station with a baby around 1.30 p.m.

A tea stall owner at the bus station recalled seeing the woman boarding a bus for Bidar. 'I particularly remember her as she was holding the baby inexpertly and was unable to stop it from crying. She looked exhausted and was walking with a limp. I told her to give the baby some milk. She was feeding such a small baby out of a bottle, which I thought was odd.'

The time by now was 6.30 p.m.

Inspector Vamsi immediately went to the manager of

the bus depot and collected the mobile numbers of the conductor and driver of the bus which had travelled to Bidar, with the woman and the child as passengers. The conductor quickly identified the WhatsApp photo sent by the police. But they were too late.

'Sir, we reached our final destination ten minutes back. She got down at the New Kaman Bus Stop some thirty minutes ago. If you had called us earlier, we could have taken her to the local police station ourselves.'

On Inspector Shiv Shankar's advice, Vamsi—accompanied by one male and one female constable—immediately started out for Bidar. The Additional Commissioner of Police, Crimes & SIT, called up her counterpart in Bidar and her request for cooperation was immediately granted. On 2 July, the Bidar police started a door-to-door search in the New Kaman Bus Stop area.

∽

Returning to my parents' home with the newborn baby nestled in my arms, I felt an odd mix of emotions. I had a baby! But I had woven a web of deceit, pretending this child was mine.

As I stepped in, the familiar warmth of my childhood home enveloped me, and my heart swelled with both joy and guilt. My parents were waiting for me, their faces radiant with anticipation. Even Genelia, my sister, seemed delighted to see me back, as was Jacob, my beloved brother. I could hardly bear to meet their joyous gazes.

When they laid their eyes on the baby for the first time, their joy was overwhelming. My parents' faces lit up with the glow of becoming grandparents, their hearts bursting with love. Genelia and Jacob took turns holding the baby, cooing and smiling at her as if she were the answer to all their dreams.

I couldn't help but share in their joy, their love and support filling me with warmth. But beneath the joy and gratitude, fear gnawed at me. What if my deception was discovered? What if the authorities traced me back here? The walls of my parents' home, once a sanctuary, now felt like they were closing in on me. At the same time, remorse would suddenly claw at my conscience whenever I let my guard down. I had stolen this baby from a new mother, someone who must be living through her own nightmare of loss. It was a cruel act, and I was well aware of the pain it must have caused her. But I suppressed my remorse with cold determination. This was the only way to save my marriage, the only way to prevent a divorce that would have shattered me.

That evening, as I rested with my sleeping baby beside me, I gazed down at that tiny, fragile bundle of life and felt an indescribable depth of love welling up within me. It was a love like no other, a love that was fierce and unyielding, a love that transcended time and space. In that instant, I knew that I would do anything, absolutely *anything* for this precious soul that had been entrusted to me.

My mother had helped me bathe the baby with warm water and I marvelled at the softness of her skin, the delicate flutter of those tiny eyelashes, and her sweet, innocent scent. Every feature, every movement, every sound this little one made felt like a miracle. I whispered promises to my baby, unbreakable promises that were etched in my heart.

'I will be here for you, my darling, through every joy and every challenge. I will nurture you, guide you, and watch you grow. I will hold you close when you need comfort and give you space to explore the world when you're ready. I will love you, not just today or tomorrow, but for all the days of my life.'

Tears of overwhelming gratitude streamed down my cheeks as I realized the incredible privilege and responsibility that had been bestowed upon me. I vowed to be the best mother I could possibly be, to provide a safe and loving home, to teach and inspire, and to be a source of unwavering support.

However, next morning, things took a sinister turn when local TV news channels started broadcasting the news of a baby kidnapped from the Government Maternity Hospital in Sultan Bazar. The CCTV footage showed me carrying a baby, and my family immediately recognized me. I tried to lie my way out of the situation. But my mother questioned how I had managed to deliver the baby and return home all by myself. I tried to explain that I had called them twice from the hospital, informing them about my plan to return after the delivery. My sister, Genelia, flatly refused to believe me, and tensions escalated. I tried my best to convince them that I had given birth to the baby in Hyderabad. But after repeated grilling, I finally broke down and admitted that the baby was not mine.

'What could I do?' I sobbed. 'My mother-in-law would have thrown me out had she known that I had miscarried. I had no other choice but to kidnap another baby to convince my in-laws to accept me.'

The TV channels reported that the police had traced me till Bidar's MG Bus Station. My parents were sure that other acquaintances in the locality would also recognize me from the CCTV footage on the TV channels and inform the police.

As panic set in, my brother, Jacob, suggested seeking help from his friend Praveen, who advised us to leave the baby at the Bidar Maternity Hospital and leave the area.

The very thought of giving Ishitha up tore me apart. I had fallen in love with that innocent baby and considered her to be my own flesh and blood. I couldn't bear to part with her. But the fear of arrest loomed like a storm on the horizon. My parents' advice weighed heavily on me. Their suggestion was like a noose around my neck, strangling my hopes of a future with Ishitha.

Late in the night, my brother took me on his bike to the hospital. With tears streaming down my face, I hugged Ishitha's tiny form one last time. I had wrapped her in shawls and tucked in a bottle of milk. I hoped she would be okay. It was a painful farewell. I felt like my soul was being torn apart as I looked at her innocent sleeping face. The hospital's porch was dimly lit and I gently placed her there, praying she would be safe.

As I walked away, each step felt like a betrayal of the

The Kidnapping of Baby Ishitha

love I had for Ishitha. The night was filled with ominous shadows and my mind raced with terrifying scenarios. What if a stray dog found her before someone else did? What if that beggar woman who often roamed near the hospital noticed Ishitha lying alone on the ground and kidnapped her with the intent of using the infant to get more money while begging?

The darkness of the night mirrored the darkness in my heart as I left her behind, praying for some guardian angel to watch over her.

While in hiding, I followed the news of the kidnapping obsessively on TV. The news channels reported that the police were investigating the case on priority. They repeatedly telecast the incriminating video as if they had no other news. I was frightened and prayed fervently to God to save me. What else could I do?

A day later, a news channel reported that the police had received information about a baby who had been abandoned at the Bidar hospital. A lady police officer, the Additional Commissioner of Police, Crimes & SIT, and her team had rushed to the hospital. The ACP personally took the baby back to Hyderabad, reuniting her with her parents. I was sad, but also relieved that the baby was finally with her mother. I said a small prayer, thanking God for listening to my desperate prayers and keeping my Ishitha safe.

In Bidar, the police worked tirelessly to trace me by showing the CCTV footage that was captured in the hospital, and with the help of a local electrician, they eventually traced me.

I was arrested in Shahgunj. Broken and remorseful, I confessed my crimes to the police, explaining that my actions were driven by desperation to save my marriage after multiple miscarriages.

Though some understood my pain, my crime could not go unpunished, and my case is now pending in court. The silver lining in this dark incident is that my husband realized his mistake and reconciled with me, expressing his love and support.

Reflecting on the ordeal, I can't help but think of Vincent van Gogh's words about hidden fires in people's souls. My inability to bear children had been a raging fire, causing immense physical and mental pain, but it remained invisible to those around me. Instead of giving me support, they fuelled the flames further with their blames and threats, leading to the unfortunate events that unfolded.

Innocence Robbed

Madhavi's Story

My name is Madhavi and I study in class II now. People say that I am a timid and withdrawn kid, too silent and mature for my age. But they haven't seen life the way I have. When I was in LKG, I used to think that the world was a lovely place. I was happy with my small family, parents and a sweet elder sister—Mahathi didi. I was close to my sister, as my mother was always busy. But I didn't mind, as my sister loved me and took care of me.

Then I got the first shock of my life. I was separated from my sister and sent off to live with my amama—my mother's mother—and maternal uncle. I didn't want to go. I cried and cried.

But amma said, 'Amama is old. Who will look after her? You are a big girl now. You need to take care of her, no?'

'But didi is older to me. Why can't she go?'

'Because she needs to take care of me, sweetheart. Who will take care of me? Don't you love your amama?'

I nodded in agreement immediately, because I loved amma and would do anything to help her.

So, I was packed off to my grandmother's place.

I was lonely at my grandmother's home.

'Your father is good for nothing! Unable to take care of his children. So he packs you off to my place. He is such a shameless bugger!' She would sneer at me.

It was then I realized that my grandmother did not need to be taken care of. I needed her, not the other way round. I was mortified. I cried myself to sleep for many nights after that. My mother did not love me enough to keep me with her. I was a burden to her. But my mother's brother, Suresh uncle, loved me. He indulged me and got me chocolates. He treated me like his own child. Gradually, I forgot my mother's rejection and started to adjust to my new family.

Suresh uncle decided that I needed a strong education and a solid background in English.

'If you know English, you will shine in life,' he would tell me seriously. 'I wish I knew more English. I could have gotten a better job with a better salary.' I would sit beside him while he had dinner after coming home from work. One day he said, 'I have found a good teacher for you. Sandhya ma'am teaches English and has a good reputation. You are going to an English-medium school. If you are not strong in English, you will not do well in your studies, *ma*!'

One good thing about my uncle was that he never treated me as a child. He always spoke to me like an equal, which made me respect and love him all the more.

I nodded eagerly. I wanted to please him and keep him happy. My grandmother, though, was not pleased with this extra expenditure.

Innocence Robbed

'English! Madhavi will learn English and become a *memsahib*!' She would taunt me. But they only made me more determined to do well.

From the next day, I started to go to Sandhya ma'am's class. She was a corpulent lady who wheezed while teaching. She was strict and would shout at kids who did not do their homework. But I never got into any trouble. I did all the tasks that she gave me. I was interested in my studies. My uncle also helped me if I had any doubts.

Sandhya ma'am often got sick and needed to visit the doctor regularly. On those days, Prabhakar sir, Sandhya ma'am's husband, would take the classes. Somehow, I never felt comfortable in his presence, though he was kind to me and gave me chocolates. Often, he would allot us some work and leave the room with my friend Lakshmi. For extra coaching, he would say. Lakshmi would resist. But he would say, 'Lakshmi, it's for your good. Come… *Come.*'

Lakshmi would come back after some time and she would be crying. I assumed that sir had punished her for not doing her homework properly. I would give her the chocolate that sir gave me and whisper to her, 'What happened? Did he beat you?' She would not respond but continue to cry silently.

I would tell her, 'Next time, do your homework properly, okay. Then he won't scold you.'

Then one day, Sandhya ma'am had gone to the doctor and Lakshmi was absent.

Sir started to scold me for no reason. I was stupefied. What had I done wrong?

Candle in the Wind

'You need some extra coaching today,' he told me sternly. He looked at the other students and said, 'Read out loud from this book. A for apple; B for bat;... Don't stop till I come back.'

When the class obediently started reading loudly, he looked at me and said, 'Come with me.'

He took me to the bathroom and did things to me which even now make me want to puke. After he was finished, he made me clean him and myself, and said, 'Don't tell anybody. Else, I will kill you! And anyway, nobody will believe you, you dirty little girl!'

I realized then what was happening to Lakshmi. Like her, I must have done something terrible. That was why I was also being punished. But what did I do wrong? I was always trying to be a good little girl.

That night, sir dropped me home. On the way, he warned me again, 'Don't tell anybody what you have done to me, okay? Only naughty girls do this sort of thing. But I will continue to love you. Here, have some chocolate.'

That night, I cried and cried. I was too ashamed to say anything to anybody. Grandma would not have believed me. And how could I even discuss such things with uncle? I felt sick and vomited.

Grandma shouted at me. 'You eat all junk food and now vomit. Clean up the mess and go to bed!'

Uncle helped me clean the mess I made, and I sank into my bed. The very thought of going for tuition the next day filled me with despair. So, the next day, when it was time for me to go for tuition, I feigned sickness.

Innocence Robbed

Grandma started shouting at me. 'My son is paying so much for the tuitions and you refuse to go? Does money grow on trees?' Despite my tears, she forcibly dropped me at the coaching centre. Prabhakar sir was waiting. When he finished with me in the bathroom, he asked, 'Did you tell anyone?'

I lowered my gaze and shook my head.

'Good girl! This will be our little secret. And you are my new wife. Keep me happy and I will see to it that you do well in class. Here, have some chocolate.'

I never knew that chocolate could taste so bitter.

This ordeal continued for fourteen days. Finally, I fell so sick and had so high a fever that my parents were sent for.

I was lying in bed when they came. Didi understands me well. She quickly sensed that something was terribly amiss. While we were alone—playing Ludo together—she asked me again if something was wrong. It was then that the entire ordeal tumbled out of my mouth.

'Didi, don't force me to go to that coaching centre,' I pleaded, in tears. 'That teacher's husband, Prabhakar uncle, is a monster. He is making me do things which I am ashamed to even think about.'

'You should have told amma!' Mahathi exclaimed, shocked and horrified.

'I was so ashamed about the whole thing!' I sobbed. 'Also, amma would think that it was all my fault. After all, she doesn't love me. That is why she sent me away to live with amama. I hate it here! Please don't tell her! Don't tell anybody. That uncle said that he would kill me if I told anybody!'

Mahathi hugged me tight. 'I will never let anything bad happen to you. Trust me. But we need to inform amma.'

When my uncle came to know about it, he went red with anger.

'I will teach that bastard a lesson,' he promised me, gathering me in his arms. Then I knew that everything would be fine. It was not my fault that these bad things happened to me. That night I slept peacefully for the first time in many days.

∞

Sandhya's Story

My name is J.D. Sandhya Rani, wife of J.D. Prabhakar. I am a graduate and used to work in a daycare centre. I was never beautiful. My parents were always worried about how they would be able to find a groom for me. After my graduation, after facing a string of rejections, I was in seventh heaven when Prabhakar and his family consented to the match. My family also rejoiced. Prabhakar had studied only till tenth standard and had a job as an office boy, but it could have been worse. I could have remained unmarried all my life.

From day one, it was apparent to me that Prabhakar was not interested in me. He was a reluctant lover, but how could I blame him? With my ugly face and fat body, how could I expect anything more? But I thought that with time I would give him so much love that he would forget my appearance and love me for myself.

Alas, that was not to be. But I had two kids, and I tried to be happy with them. Prabhakar and I started to sleep separately after the kids were born. After childbirth, I turned to food for happiness. Soon, my sugar level became so high that I had to take regular insulin injections.

Due to my poor health, I couldn't go to the daycare centre regularly. Nor could I lift the small kids and tend to them. Prabhakar's salary was not enough to bear the living and education costs of the family. I was the primary breadwinner.

I was at my wits' end, trying to make ends meet, when I came up with the idea of opening a coaching centre in our drawing room. For the first time, I saw enthusiasm in Prabhakar. He actively supported the idea of opening the coaching centre. He even promised to run it in case I fell sick. Truth be told, I could not have run the coaching centre if he hadn't helped me. I was happy for the next two years when Prabhakar and I successfully operated the coaching centre. We built a good reputation, and people began to trust us and send their kids to our centre. We were working together and also making enough money. This was the happiest phase of my married life.

Then one day, everything fell apart.

The day started normally enough. The previous day, I had gone to the doctor and was still feeling weak. Prabhakar solicitously made tea for me in the morning and even helped with the preparation of breakfast. This struck me as odd; he is usually never so considerate.

'What have you done? Why are you so nice today?' I joked.

We had just finished breakfast when I heard people shouting. At first I did not pay attention, but then they were banging on my front door as if they would break it down. My heart started thumping with fear. My sixth sense told me that it must be something to do with Prabhakar. This was confirmed when he grabbed me and whispered, 'Tell them I am not at home.' He hid himself in the bathroom.

Bracing myself for a confrontation, I opened the door.

'Where is that madarchod husband of yours?' The man at the door asked aggressively. A few more young men accompanied him. Initially, I did not recognize him. Then I realized that it was Madhavi's guardian.

'Why…? Wh-what happened?' I stammered.

'Don't you keep tabs on your husband? He has done filthy things with Madhavi. Where were you when these things happened? Where the hell is that chutiya?'

'He is not at home! And don't incriminate somebody without proof!' I have struggled a lot in my life. Toughness comes easily to me.

'Proof? I will kill the bastard when I get my hands on him.'

'My husband would never do such a thing. You are wrong. There is some sort of mistake, I am sure!' I kept repeating. Blood was pounding in my head. I could hardly understand what Madhavi's uncle was saying.

Innocence Robbed

'Where is that madarchod?' His friend demanded. 'We are going to kill him today.'

'He has gone out. And don't dare touch my husband! I will file a police complaint against you all,' I shouted.

'Arrey! We will make the police complaint. We will put that pervert in jail!' Madhavi's uncle shouted.

'Go, do whatever you can!' I shouted back, slamming the door on their faces.

I was quaking with shame and fear. The neighbours must have heard. What would they think of us? I thanked God that the kids were at school. At least they were spared the embarrassment. But no, soon the word would spread. Would anybody in this mohalla talk to us again?

I sat on the sofa, clutching my head in my hands. In my mind, I knew that my husband Prabhakar had molested the child. At that moment, I realized why he was never interested in having sex with me. I have read and heard about such men who are attracted to children, but I never realized that my husband was one such man.

Then I heard Prabhakar creeping out of the bathroom. His behaviour was a confirmation of guilt. Still, I had to be sure.

'Did you molest her, Prabhakar?' I asked without looking up at him. My head was still clutched in my hands. I was too ashamed, too repulsed to even look at him.

'No, no...of course not!' He stammered.

'You are lucky that your kids are not at home. What would they have thought of you? Now I understand why you were never interested in sleeping with me. And all the while, I blamed myself. I thought that I was lacking...that I was fat and ugly. You never thought about me, did you? You just continued to make me feel guilty, you bastard.'

'I haven't done anything!' He blustered.

'Don't lie to me, you creep! I spent so much time and effort trying to build up this coaching centre. You have ruined it all! Like a parasite, you have been eating the food that I brought to the table. And now, because of your perversion, our income will stop! What will we eat? How we will provide for the kids' school fees? Did you think about all that?'

'Trust me, I didn't do anything wrong.' He tried to take my face between his hands.

'Don't touch me!' I shouted, utterly disgusted.

I stormed into the bedroom and started to pack my bags.

'I will close this coaching centre and go to my parents with my kids. As soon as they come back from school, I am leaving. Don't come anywhere near me!' I slammed the door on his face.

That evening, I moved out and since then, I have never tried to contact him. My sons are also happy. They never received any true love from him and don't miss him. I prefer to raise them single-handedly rather than remain married to a selfish, cold-hearted paedophile.

Prabhakar's Story

My name is Prabhakar and I am about to tell you my story—a story that will leave most of you horrified. Yet, I assure you that my story will resonate with the remaining few who will smirk and be titillated by what I have done, perhaps the very thing they want to do in their deepest fantasies but don't dare to for fear of getting caught.

Perhaps you are wondering who I am. I am a middle-aged man, jailed for twenty years. Some would say I am a pervert who is being punished for pursuing a taste of my own. You see, I have a taste for young flesh—the younger, the better. But what is so perverted about it? This is what annoys me. Who says that we have to be attracted only to those of our age? Why this unwillingness among us to explore or even acknowledge an attraction that deviates from this conviction that one needs to be attracted to people of the opposite sex and that too of a similar age group. Isn't this a narrow-minded attitude to take? Why not sample pleasures from all age groups? Celebrate the full range?

As I write my notes, the prison bell rings—roll-call time. My concentration breaks as name after name is called, and they shout back their attendance. I am afraid of them—these thugs. I have been raped and beaten and treated like the scum of the earth. Yet, I don't feel that I have done anything wrong.

I really love young girls. I have always been attracted to them. Adult women turn me off. Is that a crime? I don't think so. I relate to young girls. Before my incarceration, I used to love playing with them, showering them with gifts. I touch myself as I remember those days.

Yes... Those golden days when I would gradually gain their trust by showering them with love and gifts. My wife, Sandhya, used to be impatient with these tuition kids, scolding them when they didn't do their homework. But I would make them sit on my lap and console them. Later on, when I had gained their trust and confidence, I would explore their little bodies and allow them to explore mine. What is so wrong with that? When two adults do that, it's fine. Why is it not okay when one is a child-adult, and the other a child? Yes, there is some resistance initially, but with proper grooming, coaxing and cajoling, they enjoy it. When I told them that they should not talk about our little secret to their parents as they would stop loving them, they understood.

That is what I did to most of the young girls who came to study. They all cooperated, except for Madhavi. But I don't want to remember Madhavi. She was one of my failures—a student who failed to understand the pleasures of the flesh despite my repeated attempts to groom her.

Let me not go there right now. But where should I go? To my childhood?

Childhood.

It's a mildly cold day in December. Nice and cool. My winter vacations have started. My brothers, who are a lot older than me, have gone out to play. My mother has gone to the hospital. She forever suffers from ill health. Father has gone to work. He is the sole breadwinner, responsible for feeding six mouths. I am alone in the house when the doorbell rings. It's the neighbour aunty. We all like her husband a lot. He helps us out with money and gives good advice to my father, like which school will provide more discounts to poor Catholics like us and other stuff. She comes in and asks, 'Are you alone at home?'

'Yes, mother has gone to the hospital,' I say—my voice was not yet broken by puberty.

Aunty makes sympathetic noises. 'Yes, your brothers went out to watch a movie with my sons. You poor boy, you must be feeling lonely. Come here, I will give you chocolate if you sit on my lap.'

I run to her and sit on her lap, and in the name of giving chocolate, she does unspeakable things to me. A part of me freezes. It's like I am out of my body, watching a woman of my mother's age—whom I call 'aunty'—violating my body. The woman in front of me is no longer a kindly middle-aged woman, but a lustful, dirty pervert, her features unrecognizable, distorted by lust.

After some time, she finally finishes with me. Handing me the chocolate, she says, 'If you say a word about this to anybody, I will kill your mother. Anyway, nobody will believe you.'

This abuse continued for two years. Initially, I thought it was all my fault. I was the guilty party. Once, I even tried to tell my mother. But aunty was right—my mother refused to believe me. I was shocked and hurt. It was then I realized that my mother might be kind and loving, but I could not depend on her. Later, I got habituated to the abuse. It stopped only once they moved from the neighbourhood.

But she taught me that children are the easiest possible targets. They are naïve and think that they should never tell their parents about the bad things happening to them as they would lose their love. From my own experience, I knew that most parents never believed their children.

I was not academically inclined. Also, aunty's sexual exploits turned me into a precocious child. I was rusticated from school after trying to molest a girl from a lower class, much to my parents' shame and disappointment. However, they did try to educate me. I was admitted to a different school and somehow studied till the tenth standard. After that, I refused to study any further. I started doing odd jobs, but could not stick to any particular position.

My brothers got married and moved out. I showed no interest in marriage. In fact, due to aunty's abuse, I felt nothing but revulsion for women of my age. I could not find charm and sustenance in the fully matured, past ripe, nearly sour endowments of a grown woman. Yet, I felt strangely attracted to young girls. The thought of brand-new flesh would arouse me. When my brothers had kids, I would play with them. This titillated me. Occasionally I would touch them.

How fondly do I remember Kalpana! She is my eldest brother's first child. I had groomed her oh-so-carefully. She was a pliable child. I befriended her, giving her chocolates and toys. Then gradually, I started touching and fondling her. Initially she froze, but she was a great learner and started cooperating fast. It could have continued, but her mother was very vigilant. She must have guessed something as she and Kalpana stopped coming to our house.

∞

Prison.

The ringing of bells. Dinner time. Ravi, a murderer and my protector, leers at me. He is horny. My heart sinks to my feet. Tonight will be rough. Ravi is massive—tall, dark and fat, with big bloodshot eyes. He is the strongest and most brutal of the prisoners. Initially, many of these criminals targeted me in particular; prisoners don't like child molesters. Even a murderer is treated better than a child molester. Ravi took a liking to me and decided that I would be his wife. The others then steered clear of me.

It is past midnight. Most of the prisoners are sound asleep. Ravi is impatient and excited, but I am of an age when impatience, passion and interest is more painful than exciting. He kisses me and I feel violated and repulsed. Yet, I lie quietly, enduring it all. Is this how my little lovers felt when I explored their bodies? Is it karma? He groans and grunts. The sounds he makes announce to the rest of the prisoners that I am being had again. I am the one being molested, instead of being the molester. This is retribution, a punishment. But do I deserve such punishment?

Just like those kids, I will feel him in me longer than he will feel me around him. He will put on his pants and walk off, and I will lie here on the dirty, rough floor, smelling the disgusting smell from the toilet nearby, feeling physically split in half. To escape the sordidness, I relive my memories of another toilet where I had had sex. There I was the man and a little girl was my wife. But that toilet was so much cleaner. Do I deserve this degradation? This unwarranted violence? I am sure that the little girl was never as traumatized as I am now.

༄

Adulthood, before Prison.

I am at home, having lunch lovingly cooked for me by my mother.

'Prabhakar, now that you have a steady job, you should get married,' my mother says as she serves me food.

It is Sunday, a holiday for me. I have been working as an office boy in a reputed hospital for quite some time now. My brothers are married and have moved out. I visit prostitutes and specifically ask for young girls. Life is fine. I am not inclined to get married as mature women hold no attraction for me.

'Why do you want me to get married, amma? I am happy with you.'

My mother sighs. 'You know that I am not well. Cancer is not something that gets cured. I want to see you married and settled before I die.'

So, despite my reluctance, I get married. I do my duty and my wife gets pregnant. We have two sons in rapid succession. My duty is done. So I stop sleeping with her. I continue to visit prostitutes. After a few years of marriage, my wife grows disgustingly fat and develops diabetes. Soon, she is forced to quit her job. I feel disgusted with her. I don't even like the kids. The family only talks about food, food and more food.

'Where will the food come from? Your mother is too fat to work!' I taunt them.

'Why can't you try to earn some more? Even a rickshaw puller earns more than you!' My eldest son screams back. I beat the shit out of him.

After a few months of hardship, my wife proposes opening a coaching centre for kids till class V. She is a graduate and can take care of teaching.

I am delighted with the proposal. Finally, I will get access to delicious little girls again. I agree to help her. Initially I am cautious and patient. We need to build a good reputation so that parents trust us.

Soon we get enough students. I help my wife. Her

diabetes has worsened and she needs regular medical attention. I am solicitous. I assure her that I will take good care of the kids while she is away.

For my first girl-wife, I target little Suhani. She is a motherless five-year-old girl. Her stepmother resents her and is happy to send her away for a few hours. Suhani is starved for love. I mollycoddle her and gain her trust. After six months, I get my reward when she kisses my penis. I have numerous such success stories.

But Madhavi... I met my nemesis in Madhavi. She was staying away from her parents, with her maternal uncle. So, I took the poor, neglected child under my wings. But when I asked her to kiss me and fondle me, she refused. What an ungrateful child! After all the love and attention that I showered on her. Anyway, I thought that after some initial resistance, Madhavi would begin to cooperate. But even after two weeks of grooming, she resisted. And then she stopped coming.

Initially, I was apprehensive. I had an inkling that she would confide in someone. I was prepared to defend myself. I would stoutly deny all the allegations. After all, who would believe a chit of a girl like her?

But there I was, over-optimistic. The girl's family came to confront us. I quickly hid in the bathroom, allowing my wife to face their wrath. To her credit, she staunchly supported me in front of them. But she blasted me when they left.

'I will close this coaching centre and go to my parents with my kids. As soon as they come back from school,

I am leaving. Don't come anywhere near me!' She said as she slammed the door on my face.

I thought it would be a blessing in disguise if she left with the kids for the time being. I planned to lock the door and abscond as soon as she left.

Unfortunately for me, the police arrived promptly, before I could abscond.

I was arrested and taken into police custody. At that time, I was still unsure how seriously these accusations would be taken. My worst fears were realized when the head of the police station, ACP K. Srinivasa Rao, interrogated me himself.

I am a non-violent person. The moment they questioned me harshly, I confessed to everything.

I tried to explain that what I did was not wrong because I gave the little girls special love. The police laughed at me, called me names, and said callously, 'Explain all this to the other inmates when you meet them in jail. They reserve special treatment for child molesters.'

I wet my pants.

*

Courtroom.

The judge is a fierce-looking old woman. She glares at me. I look back, poker-faced. One can easily guess whose side of the story she believes. My court-appointed lawyer is absent. He seems to be ashamed of me. He hasn't met me at all. Nobody seems to be bothered that there is no one available to defend me. Life is so unfair. I am remanded to judicial custody without further ado. Since the time I have been incarcerated, nobody has come to visit me.

༄

Suresh's Story

Madhavi is crying. She has a high fever and has been vomiting for the past few days.

She is asking for her mother and sister, but my mother refuses to inform them. 'If they come down and stay for a few days, extra money will have to be spent. You barely earn enough to take care of Madhavi and me. How can you afford to have guests?'

'We will manage. Let's just get her mother here,' I plead with her.

I feel so sad for Madhavi. She is such a sweet, innocent kid. I love her a lot! She has brought illumination to my otherwise tedious and boring life. I pray to God that she recovers soon.

Finally, as Madhavi's condition worsens, my mother grows concerned. She asks me to send for Madhavi's mother, my sister Kaveri. However, Kaveri doesn't seem very concerned. As she continues to delay her visit, I lose patience. I call and scold her, 'Your younger daughter is sick and crying for you! Can't you come and visit her even once? Don't blame me if her condition deteriorates.'

Finally, she comes along with her elder daughter, Mahathi. Madhavi is close to her sister. She is happy to see her.

'Your precious daughter is refusing to go to tuition classes. Can you find out why she is wasting money like this?' My mother complains to Kaveri.

'I asked her, amma. She refuses to tell,' Kaveri tells her. She turns to Mahathi. 'You are the only one Madhavi listens to. Why don't you explain to her that she needs to attend her tuition classes regularly if she wants to do well?' Mahathi is older than Madhavi by six years and hence is more mature. She promises to speak to Madhavi.

That evening, she sits by Madhavi's bedside and engages her in a game of Ludo. And that is when she confides in her.

∞

Once I came to know about Madhavi's ordeal, I went to the teacher Sandhya ma'am's home, along with a few friends. When the teacher refused to believe Madhavi's story, I filed a police complaint.

Even I was surprised by the promptness of the police response. Within hours, Prabhakar was arrested and taken into custody. The head of the Lalaguda Police Station, ACP K. Srinivasa Rao, took personal charge of the case.

A female police constable accompanied Madhavi and her mother to the Bharosa Centre, where her statement was recorded. Next, she was sent for a medical examination. Simultaneously, the accused, Prabhakar, was sent for a potency test.

A district magistrate recorded a 164 statement—a special statement recorded directly by the district magistrate. No other person would be present during the interview. As the child was less than six years old, she could not explain the incident adequately. A dildo was provided to her and she had to demonstrate what sexual acts were perpetrated on her. It was mortifying for her and her family, but the government ensured complete privacy and dignity for the family, and the actual statement was recorded behind closed doors.

The Hyderabad Police were incredibly diligent and ensured that all documentation—like birth certificate, potency certificate, and so on—were obtained.

A special court tried Prabhakar's case under POCSO (Protection of Children from Sexual Offences) Act, 2012, a comprehensive law to protect children from offences of sexual assault, harassment and pornography, while safeguarding their interests at every stage of the judicial process by incorporating child-friendly mechanisms for reporting, recording of evidence, investigation, and a speedy trial through designated special courts. During the trial, Madhavi could see the accused through CCTV live recordings, but no member of the public could see her. Her case was treated with extreme sensitivity by the Hyderabad Police, and they ensured that justice was delivered. The perpetrator was given a twenty-year (rigorous imprisonment) sentence, which he is currently serving.

Unrequited Love

Account of ACP, Crimes & SIT

I was in a meeting, discussing a case with my team about a woman who had been killed by her parents for eloping with her lover from a different caste. In the middle of the meeting, Constable Bhanu called me. He was excited and nervous.

'Ma'am, a serious incident has happened near the Gandipet MeeSeva Centre. A man has slit the throat of his girlfriend and is now threatening to kill himself. A crowd has gathered and is on the verge of lynching the man. What should I do?'

I rushed to the scene with my team, which included my trusted aide, P. Ashok. We found a bearded man tied to a tree and surrounded by an angry crowd. His white shirt was soaked in blood and he was in a sorry state indeed. His face was swollen and his lips were bleeding. It was evident that some men from the crowd had already assaulted him. Constable Bhanu was doing a commendable job, trying to handle the unruly crowd single-handedly.

I could see no sign of the girl the man had purportedly killed. 'Where is the girl?' I asked Constable Bhanu.

'Ma'am, the owner of the MeeSeva Centre took her to the hospital. I just got a call from him that she died on the way. I have asked the hospital authorities to keep the body in the morgue.'

I was impressed at Constable Bhanu's efficiency and made a mental note to ensure that he was suitably rewarded.

My team quickly calmed the crowd and arrested the man whose name, I gathered, was Karthik Reddy. The man was behaving like a raving lunatic and kept crying that he wanted to die. He wailed the name of Jaya and repeatedly banged his head on the trunk of the tree. We took him to the police station for questioning.

He kept saying that he used to love the girl and had killed her accidentally. I have no sympathy for these kinds of violent misogynists who kill the women they can't get, even if they pretend to show remorse afterwards. After he was locked up in police custody, I handed over the case to Ashok.

'Ensure that the man is punished for what he has done. Narcissistic and sadistic men like him should never be allowed to roam free. Let us make a watertight case against him. We should try to get capital punishment for this bastard.'

∞

Karthik's mother, Aruna, begged her rich sister Vidya to pay

Unrequited Love

for the best defence lawyer available—a shrewd man named Gangadhar Pantham. Vidya was very close to Aruna and loved her dearly.

'My useless son will die unless a good lawyer represents him, didi. I have heard that this Gangadhar has saved many criminals. And my son is a sweet innocent boy, who simply made a grave mistake. I am sure Gangadhar would be able to prove that my Karthik didn't kill that girl Jaya. Please save him, didi, I beg of you,' Aruna pleaded, shedding copious tears.

'Karthik deserves what he gets!' Her elder sister said sternly.

'But I am a mother! How can I let him hang! This money is peanuts for you. Anyway, I promise to pay back every penny. I will sell my jewellery and my house if needed,' Aruna wailed.

Finally, Vidya relented and they decided to pay Gangadhar Pantham a visit.

'This is how we will present our case to the lawyer.'

When Aruna explained how she wanted to present their side of the story to the lawyer, Vidya was shocked. 'But Aruna, we can't malign a dead girl like this. She was a rather nice girl, you know. Very punctual and sincere.'

Aruna said, 'Now is not the time for such guilty feelings, didi. It doesn't matter what kind of girl Jaya really was. She is dead. But my Karthik is alive and has his whole life ahead of him. We have to save him somehow.'

Candle in the Wind

At a small, well-appointed office within a prestigious law firm, Vidya and Aruna uneasily occupied two chairs opposite Mr Gangadhar Pantham. Vidya had to pay ₹10,000 as consultation fee before they were allowed to enter his chamber.

Gangadhar sized up the two women with practised eye. He immediately realized from Aruna's red swollen eyes that she was the person who required a lawyer.

'What happened exactly?' He asked her, after the initial greetings.

'My son, Karthik, has been arrested by the police for the murder of a girl named Jaya. But I assure you, sir, that Karthik is a very gentle person. H-he is incapable of killing *anybody*,' Aruna said, wiping her eyes.

Gangadhar waited for a few moments, allowing Aruna to regain her composure. Then he asked gently, 'Then why did the police arrest him?'

'Sir, my sister Vidya here,' she waved her hands towards Vidya, 'she owns a MeeSeva where this girl used to work. Jaya pretended to fall in love with my Karthik. I don't know what *jadu tona* she did to my son. However, on a certain day when my sister was unwell and couldn't attend office, Jaya stole ₹10,000. Karthik noticed that the money was missing from the drawer the next day. But somehow, she convinced Karthik not to tell didi. She promised that she would return the money at the end of the month. Instead, she took her salary at the end of the month and disappeared. Didi of course blamed Karthik. My Karthik was so upset that the girl had conned him into believing her.'

'When did this happen?' Gangadhar asked.

'A-about six months back.'

'Then what happened?'

'Karthik kept searching for her and finally found out that she was currently working in a MeeSeva in Gandipet. The owner of this MeeSeva had contacted my didi for a reference check.'

Gangadhar looked at Vidya. 'So you told the owner that Jaya had stolen ₹10,000?'

Vidya looked uncomfortable. She stammered, 'N-no.'

'Why not?' Gangadhar asked. To him, the story was sounding more and more fishy.

Aruna responded quickly. 'Jaya had called my didi and promised to return the amount. My didi is a very generous person. She didn't want to ruin Jaya's career. So she gave a good reference. Isn't that correct, didi?' Aruna nudged Vidya.

Vidya nodded, somewhat reluctantly. 'Yes, I didn't want to ruin her career,' she said.

'Hmmm... What happened then?'

'Karthik was upset when didi told him that she gave a good reference for Jaya even though she had duped her. He went to the Gandipet MeeSeva and confronted her about the money. When he did that, Jaya became violent. She whipped out a knife and tried to attack him. There was a struggle and he accidentally slit her throat. By this time, a crowd had gathered. When Karthik realized what he had done, he tried to slit his own throat! But some people in the crowd stopped him. Otherwise my son would have killed himself on that day only.' Aruna started to weep silently.

'So, there are many eyewitnesses to this incident.' Gangadhar commented.

Aruna nodded. 'Yes, but they did not know that she had whipped out the knife. They think that the knife belonged to my son. My son is innocent, sir. That *girl*! That girl came at a very inauspicious time in his life. She has ruined his life now. She took advantage of my son's innocence. Tell him, didi, isn't it true?' Again, she prodded her sister and Vidya nodded stonily.

Gangadhar was an experienced, shrewd lawyer. Something about Aruna's story and Vidya's body language struck him as odd. So he didn't commit himself to taking up the case immediately.

'Did the police register an FIR?' He asked.

Aruna nodded. 'Yes, Jaya's mother filed an FIR. She lied about everything, sir. She said that my Karthik had been stalking Jaya and killed her because she rejected his advances. But this is a lie!'

'Okay, let me check the FIR first. Why don't we meet in two days?' Gangadhar said.

After the two women left, Gangadhar charged his assistant Varun with finding out more details about the case.

'Dig deep. There's something wrong about this story. This doesn't pass the smell test.'

Gangadhar was on good terms with the SHO of the Gandipet Police Station. So when Varun went to meet him, the police readily cooperated. After Varun returned with the details, Gangadhar was shocked.

'This will be a really difficult case to win. This guy is

crazy! Why did he have to do all this in a public place like a MeeSeva Centre? Oh my God!'

Two days later, the two women came to meet Gangadhar.

On Gangadhar's desk lay a file with all the relevant information about the case.

As soon as they entered, he thundered, 'You lied to me! I can't take up this case!'

Aruna started to weep. 'Sir, we didn't lie! Please believe us.'

'Well, the police and the eye witnesses tell a different story. They say that the knife was Karthik's and he was the aggressor. He killed the girl.'

'Sir, there is no proof that the knife belonged to Karthik, is there?' Aruna said desperately. 'The crowd didn't notice what had happened initially.'

Gangadhar looked at Aruna sharply. He said flatly, 'Look, you have to tell me the truth. Unless I know the truth, I can't take up this case. Whatever you tell me will stay within the four walls of this office.'

Aruna covered her face with her hands and rocked herself for a minute as she thought desperately about what to do. Then she spoke up. 'Sir, Karthik was really in love with the girl. But she obviously didn't care for him. Instead, she used his weakness for her to steal money from my sister and ran away. So, when he came to know that she had taken up a job in the Gandipet MeeSeva, he went to confront her. He was angry. His ego was hurt. But I am sure that he had no intention of killing her.'

Gangadhar nodded approvingly. Aruna seemed to be finally telling the truth.

Gangadhar told her, 'Ma'am, I have thoroughly examined your case and I must be frank with you. The charge of murder your son faces is serious. The evidence against him is overwhelming. He committed this crime in broad daylight before numerous witnesses, and even confessed to the authorities. There exists no doubt as to his guilt.'

Aruna said, 'Karthik loved her! She was his life! She dumped him out of the blue and crushed his heart. Can you blame him for getting angry at her? But of course he had no intention of killing this girl. It was an accident. He is a hot-headed, foolish young man. We have to save him somehow.' She started to weep.

Gangadhar shifted uneasily in his seat. 'Ma'am, please compose yourself. I empathize with your emotions, but they hold little relevance in the court. The court concerns itself solely with facts and the law. The fact is, your son committed a heinous crime, and the law insists on appropriate punishment.'

Vidya said, 'Sir, there must be some way to salvage the situation. He is my sister's only child. She will go mad if anything happens to him. You must save him.'

Gangadhar said, 'There are two potential avenues of defence we may explore. However, I must caution you that both are exceedingly risky and offer scant chances of success.'

Aruna asked eagerly, 'What are these options?'

'Well, the first is the insanity line of defence. We can

argue that Karthik was of unsound mind at the time of the incident—that a mental disorder impaired his comprehension of the act's nature and consequences. But the problem with this option is that we have to show that he was seeing a psychiatrist for some time and he has mental issues.'

Vidya asked, 'What's the second option?'

'We can raise the issue of Jaya trying to take advantage of Karthik's weakness for her, stealing the money and then running away. But in my opinion, pleading insanity is a better option. For that, we need to show a history of insanity. If we have some medical records that he was mentally unsound and was seeing a psychiatrist…'

Aruna said eagerly, 'We can bribe a doctor and procure fake medical rec…' She stopped as she saw anger on Gangadhar's face.

Gangadhar said harshly, 'The court will not accept just any doctor's certificate. It has to be a doctor from an approved government hospital. And do you know the consequences of being found out? I can't do such illegal things. Do you know what will happen if we are caught? All of us will be in jail along with your son! My licence to practice will be suspended! I'll not take up this case if you talk like this!'

Vidya said hurriedly, 'Please forgive my sister. She's going mad trying to extricate her son from this horrible mess that he has got himself into. She is not thinking clearly.'

Gangadhar appeared mollified. 'I'm not taking offence for this time. But please don't ask me to collude with you in any illegal activities.'

Vidya said, 'Sir, you please suggest something. How can we plead insanity?'

Gangadhar sighed. 'Okay, I know a psychiatrist at Gandhi Hospital. As it is a government hospital, if he certifies that your son is mentally unstable, then we might have a fighting chance.'

'But my Karthik is in jail. How can he go and see the doctor?'

'I have contacts. I can ask the doctor to check on Karthik. But it will cost money.'

Aruna looked beseechingly at Vidya. Vidya sighed.

'How much?'

Gangadhar named a sum. Vidya looked at Aruna's face and sighed again. She agreed to pay the amount. 'But will the doctor certify that Karthik is legally insane?'

'I can't guarantee that. The doctor is an honest person. He will give us the truth. I would suggest that you ask Karthik to pretend insanity. Maybe he can convince the doctor.'

Aruna nodded, 'I am visiting him in jail tomorrow. I'll coach him.'

Gangadhar got up from his seat, indicating that the meeting was over. He said, 'Let me organize this. I request you to meet me again in a week's time. My secretary will call you and fix an appointment.'

∞

A week later, Gangadhar met with the two women again.

'I have bad news. The doctor says that Karthik is sane. There is no way we can plead legal insanity.'

Aruna sighed. 'You had mentioned about the second option…'

Vidya squirmed uneasily in her seat.

Gangadhar said, 'Yes, as I mentioned before, the second option involves asserting that Jaya pilfered funds from you when she was working at the MeeSeva Centre you owned. According to this narrative, Karthik pursued her to reclaim the money and, in a fit of rage, she assaulted him. Consequently, in the ensuing struggle, he took Jaya's life accidentally.' He looked at Vidya. 'You will need to take the witness stand and confirm the story.'

Vidya sighed. 'I will corroborate our story.'

Gangadhar nodded. 'The aim is to establish an alternative motive for Karthik's actions and to shift some culpability onto Jaya.' He rubbed his hands briskly. 'We must unearth evidence implicating Jaya—surveillance videos, bank statements or credible eyewitness accounts.'

Vidya said, 'Sir, such evidence does not exist. I don't have a CCTV camera in my office.'

Aruna said, 'But your accountant can show an unexplained deficit of ₹10,000 in the ledger. Didi, you can tell the court that you realized Jaya had taken money from the cash counter in the MeeSeva Centre when you were doing the accounts. Later, you grilled her and she confessed to the crime and promised to return the money. Please, didi, please help us.'

Gangadhar nodded approvingly, 'Yes, and we can say

that she quit the MeeSeva Centre without returning the money, and Karthik was following up with her to recover it. But we have to mention that they had an affair when she worked at your MeeSeva Centre. Because he confessed during his initial arrest that he loved her. We can say she argued with him and refused to return the money. We can also present that she tried to attack him with a knife and, in the ensuing struggle, she was killed. That way, he may be convicted only for second-degree manslaughter and walk away with a maximum of five years' imprisonment.'

Vidya looked terrified. 'I have to lie in court because I have no real proof that she took the money.'

'Your accountant pointed out the deficit in the ledger, no?' Gangadhar asked. 'That'll be enough.'

Aruna said, 'Please, didi. You are like a mother to him. If your own son were in this situation, you would have done your best, no? Please, didi, how can we be caught! This is the only way out.'

Vidya ignored Aruna. Instead, she asked Gangadhar, 'Sir, do we really have to tell the world that she stole money from me? I have no real proof that she took the money. The maid who dusted the office could also have taken it. I will tell you the truth. When I had confronted Jaya about the money, she swore to me that she never took the money. And I had no reason to disbelieve her, as she had been very trustworthy, efficient and punctual otherwise.'

Gangadhar told Vidya gently, 'We have to project that Jaya stole the money and ran away. Otherwise, there is no possible defence. Just think, ma'am. Not only will Karthik be convicted of murder, but he may even face capital punishment.'

Aruna started to weep. 'Oh Lord! Oh merciful Venkateshwara! I feel dizzy!'

Vidya said desperately, 'Can't we plead insanity?'

Gangadhar shook his head. 'Not possible, ma'am. There is no medical history of insanity. And the government doctor has pronounced that he is mentally fit for a normal trial. This is our only option. We have to show her as a thief and a person who tried to take advantage of Karthik's love. That is the best way.'

Vidya looked uncomfortable. But Aruna said hurriedly, 'Thank you, sir. I, too, feel this is the best way to proceed.'

Gangadhar said briskly, 'Very well, then. We will start the legal work. The trial commences soon, and we need to be prepared with our defence. You will need to pay additional money for the legal work that we will be doing. But I must warn you. He will most probably be sentenced for life.'

'Sentenced for life?' Aruna paled.

'Don't worry, ma'am. In our Indian courts, sentenced for life means eleven years in jail, that's all. And if he behaves well, he will be out even earlier. We have too many criminals and too few jails. What I will ensure is that he doesn't get death penalty,' Gangadhar said grimly.

After they came back home, Vidya said, 'Jaya is a nice girl, you know. She never stole any money.'

Aruna said, 'Didi, don't talk like this in public. We have to convince your accountant to produce this fake ledger deficit. Please, didi, Karthik's life is at stake here. And we must never tell Gangadhar garu that Jaya didn't steal any money. Else, he won't defend Karthik. Please, didi. You too love Karthik like your own son, don't you? What will happen to me if Karthik is hanged? He made a mistake. But we have to save him.'

Vidya's face contorted in anger. She shouted, 'What Karthik did to that girl was despicable. But only for your sake, I will lie in court. Though what will happen if they catch me…have you ever thought of that?'

Aruna fell to the ground and grasped Vidya's feet with both hands. 'Please, didi. You are my God. Only you can save my child. I know what Karthik did was wrong. *Baabu… Chinna pillavaadu. Dayachesi athanni shaminchandi. Athanni kaapaadandi*, please, didi… He is just a child, please forgive him and save him!' She wept uncontrollably.

Vidya's face softened. 'Get up, Aruna. I'll see what I can do. But I'm doing this only for your sake.'

∞

The Trial

The prosecution lawyer, Mr Bhaskar Kumar, and Mr Gangadhar Pantham were already at the table in the courtroom when the police escorted a handcuffed Karthik in. The court was packed with people, with all the seats taken and the remaining people standing at the back. The press had milked the juicy story of two young lovers to the fullest, inciting public interest.

'All rise,' said the court clerk, a mousy, slim man. He was wearing a white cotton shirt and black pants that had seen better days.

Judge Sukesh Buka arrived and took his seat. After making himself comfortable, he intoned, 'In the matter of "Jaya Bachu vs Karthik Reddy" on this date of 15 September 2018, what does the prosecutor have to say?' He put on his half-moon reading glasses and swiftly perused the file before him, nodding to himself as he read.

'Your Honour, we are ready to proceed,' Mr Kumar said, standing up.

'And how about the defence?'

'We are ready too, Your Honour.'

'Let the proceedings commence then.'

The prosecutor then presented his opening statement.

'Your Honour, Karthik Reddy is a dangerous man. He made Jaya's life miserable when she was his girlfriend. She couldn't bear his constant abuse and decided to leave him. Even then, he pursued her relentlessly. His ego was hurt that she rejected him.'

He continued in this vein and gave a powerful picture of a young, unruly and violent man stalking a helpless female. He concluded by saying, 'Your Honour, he allegedly tried to commit suicide after killing Jaya, but he never really intended to kill himself. He just wanted to fool the world into believing that he never really intended to kill the victim and was remorseful. But he knew that the public would prevent him from committing suicide. If a person really intends to kill himself, he wouldn't choose such a busy public place to do so. It is clear that he went to meet the girl with only one motive. He wanted to kill her because she had hurt his ego by rejecting his advances. He wanted revenge. His attitude was: "If I can't have you, then nobody else can." He is an immature, possessive psychopath. I have presented the note that he had written as evidence. Jaya was a sweet, innocent girl who was killed in the prime of her life, and justice must prevail. That's all, Your Honour.'

'Mr Pantham, do you want to make your opening statement now?'

'Your Honour,' Gangadhar Pantham rose from the defence table. 'We don't want this to be a trial full of histrionics. The prosecution has presented the case very soberly without going into salacious details and we sincerely thank them for that. If nothing else, let's start from the presumption that the defendant, Mr Karthik Reddy here, never intended to kill Ms Jaya. Presumption of innocence till proven guilty is the birthright of every Indian citizen.' After this initial courtesy to the prosecuting lawyer, Mr Pantham made a brief opening statement where he tried to project that Karthik had no love interest in Jaya and was simply pursuing her for the money she had stolen from his aunt. Mr Pantham stood silent for a minute after concluding his opening statement. Then he added, 'That's all, Your Honour.'

∞

Judge Buka considered for a minute, then said, 'Mr Bhaskar Kumar, please call your first witness to the stand.'

'Yes, Your Honour. I would like to call the Additional Commissioner of Police, Crimes & SIT, who made the arrest.'

The ACP had a commanding presence, with fair complexion and blue eyes. As she walked up to the witness stand, she exuded grace, her upright posture conveying a sense of confidence and poise. After the ACP had stated her full name and designation, the prosecutor began to ask questions which she answered precisely, her words carrying weight and resonance.

She explained how a constable near the scene of crime had initially witnessed the crime and informed her. She had then arrived at the scene of crime herself, along with the station head of Gandipet Police Station, and made the arrest. She then explained that she appointed a team headed by Additional Superintendent of Police P. Ashok as the investigation officer. The team recorded the statements of the people at the scene of crime, who had witnessed the struggle between the victim and the killer. The owner of the MeeSeva Centre had witnessed the killer actually drawing the knife across the throat of the victim. His statement too had been recorded by the police.

'Mr Pantham?' Asked Judge Buka.

'The defence has no questions for this witness at this time, Your Honour.'

Next, the prosecution called Dr Laxman, who had performed the autopsy, to the witness stand.

Dr Laxman was a tall, elderly man who had conducted several autopsies for the Hyderabad Police. He looked confident and self-assured. He took the oath and responded to Mr Kumar's questions regarding his qualifications and professional experience in a bored voice.

'In your expert opinion, Dr Laxman, how did the victim die?' Mr Kumar pointed to the photo of the victim taken by a reporter who had been having tea near the scene of crime when the murder took place. The photo was projected on the screen placed next to the prosecutor's desk. The next slide showed the victim lying on the autopsy table. Very cleverly, the public prosecutor had given a glimpse of the dead girl to the judge and the public. The objective was to make things real and to garner public sympathy for the girl whose life had been tragically cut short in its prime. Jaya's mother started to weep on seeing the photos.

Dr Laxman deposed that he had conducted the postmortem examination of Jaya and found a deeply incised wound on the right side of the neck, involving the carotid arteries and the external jugular vein. These injuries were anti-mortem in nature.

The prosecutor raised the knife, the murder weapon, in its plastic bag and asked, 'Could this knife have been used to make the injuries that caused the death?'

Dr Laxman nodded emphatically. 'Yes, the knife could certainly have been lethal.'

'We have no further questions for this witness, Your Honour,' announced Mr Kumar.

'Mr Pantham?' Asked Judge Buka.

'The defence has no questions for the witness at this time, Your Honour.'

'You may step down, Dr Laxman.'

Dr Laxman removed himself from the witness stand.

'Let's take a break now and return after lunch. The court is now in recess until 2.00 p.m.' Judge Buka got up to leave.

After lunch, the prosecution called in their next witness—Srikanth Reddy, the son of the owner of the MeeSeva Centre where Jaya had been working when she was killed.

The courtroom was tense as the prosecutor walked up to the witness stand. He looked at the witness, a young man with black hair and a trimmed moustache, dressed in blue shirt and trousers. He wore spectacles and looked like a serious, nerdy kind of person.

'Please state your name and occupation for the record,' the prosecutor said.

'My name is Srikanth Reddy. My father owns the MeeSeva Centre in Gandipet,' the witness replied.

'What were you doing there?'

'Sir, I work there.'

'So, you were Jaya's colleague at the MeeSeva Centre?'

'Yes, sir.'

'Thank you, Mr Reddy. Now, can you tell us what you saw on the morning of 10 July 2021?'

'Yes, I can. I was working at my desk at the MeeSeva Centre, when I heard a loud scream. I looked out of the window and saw a man holding a knife to Jaya's neck. He looked very furious and violent. Jaya was crying and pleading with him to stop. She tried to pull away from him, but he was too strong. I ran to help Jaya. But by the time I reached her, she had collapsed to the ground, bleeding heavily. It all happened so quickly! I was shocked and horrified.'

'Did you recognize the man?'

'No, I didn't know him at the time.'

'So, you didn't know that he had been her lover and was stalking her after she broke up with him due to his abusive behaviour?' the prosecutor asked.

'Objection, Your Honour. There is no proof that they were lovers! And there is no proof that he was abusive,' Mr Pantham interrupted.

'Objection sustained. Strike off the last statement from the record. And Mr Kumar, please refrain from making any loose statements.'

'Okay, let me rephrase the question. Did you get to know about this man later?'

'Yes, I did. The man was Karthik Reddy. After killing Jaya, he shouted that he and Jaya had been lovers and he killed her because she rejected his marriage proposal.'

There was an uproar in the court.

'Order! Order!' Judge Buka said, rapping his gavel on his desk.

'Did you or anyone else call the police or try to help Jaya?'

'Yes, I alerted my father and then ran outside to help Jaya. My father tried to stop Jaya's bleeding while I was struggling with Karthik to prevent him from slashing his own throat. Then, other people, who were having chai in a nearby shop, saw me struggle with Karthik and helped me subdue him. We tied him to a tree. Meanwhile, my father was trying to stop Jaya's bleeding with a scarf. There was so much blood everywhere.'

'Objection, Your Honour,' Mr Pantham shouted. He could see that the audience was getting agitated as Srikanth described the gory scene. He guessed that the judge was similarly affected. 'Srikanth did not see the actual murder happening. Where is the proof that my client actually pulled the knife and cut Jaya's throat? I present that Jaya had attacked my client with a knife, and he seized the knife and then accidentally cut her throat while trying to defend himself. There is no proof that the accused had a knife with him when the struggle happened.'

'Your Honour, there are many witnesses who saw the accused whip out the knife from his pocket and slash the girl's throat.'

'Objection overruled. The witness may continue,' Judge Buka said.

Mr Kumar asked, 'Before you continue…did the accused, Mr Karthik, seriously try to kill himself?'

'Objection, Your Honour!' The defence lawyer yelled. 'There were many witnesses who were there. If they had not physically restrained the accused, he would have committed suicide on that day. He felt so guilty after he accidentally injured the victim that he immediately tried to take his own life.'

'Objection sustained.'

Mr Kumar said to the witness, 'So Mr Srikanth, you were telling us about how you caught the accused and how the victim's throat was slashed.'

Srikanth Reddy continued, 'She had a faint pulse. My father hailed an auto and rushed her to the hospital. But at the hospital, they told him that she was already dead.' The horror of the moment was reflected on Srikanth's face as he revisited the experience in court. There was a murmur in the audience. They sympathized with the victim. They looked at the accused with loathing. Karthik himself avoided looking at anybody. He sat stone-faced and stared at the ground. The prosecutor had done an excellent job projecting Karthik as a cold-blooded killer.

'I'm sorry, Mr Reddy. That must have been very traumatic for you.'

'It was. I still can't believe it happened.'

'Thank you for your testimony, Mr Reddy. You have been very courageous and helpful. No further questions, Your Honour.'

The prosecutor nodded at the judge and returned to his seat. The defence lawyer, Mr Pantham, rose from his seat and approached the witness stand.

Mr Pantham smiled at the witness, but his eyes were sharp and cunning. 'Mr Reddy, are you sure that you saw what you say you saw?' He asked.

'Yes, I am sure. I saw Jaya lying on the ground, blood everywhere. I will never forget that sight,' Srikanth said.

'Are you sure it was Karthik? Did you see his face clearly?'

'Yes, I did. He was wearing a red shirt and blue jeans. He had a distinctive voice. And he had the same tall and athletic build. It was him, alright.'

'Did you see the knife clearly? What kind of knife was it?'

'It was a medium-sized knife, like a kitchen knife. It had a silver blade and a black handle. It was very sharp.'

'Did you see where he got the knife from? Did he have it with him or did he pick it up from somewhere?'

'I don't know. I didn't see him take out the knife. He just had it in his hand when he attacked Jaya.'

'So, you don't know if he brought the knife with him or if he snatched it from Jaya's hands in self-defence?'

Srikanth hesitated, then said, 'No, I don't.'

'Is it possible that he took the knife from Jaya and used it in a moment of self-defence?'

'I don't think so. He seemed to be aware of what he was doing. He didn't hesitate or regret his action.'

'How do you know that? Did you see his expression or hear him say anything?'

'Yes, I did. He still looked angry. He said something like, "You betrayed me, Jaya. You deserve to die." He sounded very bitter and hateful.'

'Did you hear what Jaya said to him? Did she say anything that could have provoked him or made him angry?'

'I heard what she said. She was just crying and begging for her life. She said something like, "Please, Karthik, don't do this." She sounded very scared.'

'So, you don't know what their relationship was like? You don't know if they had any problems or conflicts?'

'No, I don't. That was the first time I came to know about this Karthik and how he had been constantly harassing her and trying to force her to marry him.'

'Is it possible that they had some issues that you were not aware of? Did you know that she had stolen money from Karthik's aunt's MeeSeva Centre and that he was following up with her to get the money back?'

Srikanth Reddy shook his head. 'I didn't know. Maybe. But that doesn't justify killing her in such a brutal manner.'

'Of course not, Mr Reddy. I'm not trying to justify Karthik's actions. I'm just trying to understand his motives and state of mind. You see, Mr Reddy, Karthik is not a cold-blooded killer. He is a human being who made a terrible mistake in a moment of self-defence. He was Jaya's classmate and friend. He got her a job at his aunt's MeeSeva Centre. But how did she respond? She tried to cheat, and bit the very hand that fed her. He felt betrayed and hurt by her actions. He snapped and lost control of himself. He regrets what happened and he is sorry for what he did to Jaya and her family. He is not a monster, Mr Reddy. He is a victim of his own emotions.'

Mr Kumar interjected, 'Objection, Your Honour. Mr Pantham has no proof that Jaya did anything wrong.'

The defence lawyer looked at the judge with an injured expression. 'I have proof, Your Honour! I would like to call my next witness, Ms Vidya, Mr Karthik's aunt, who owns the MeeSeva Centre where Jaya used to work.'

Vidya was called to the witness stand where she testified that Jaya had stolen ₹10,000 from the MeeSeva Centre on the day she had been alone because Vidya was sick.

The prosecution asked if she could provide any proof.

The defence produced printouts of her accounts which showed a supposed mismatch of ₹10,000.

The prosecution promptly ripped the defence witness apart. 'The witness cannot be trusted as she is the aunt of the accused. Secondly, assuming that it's true that Jaya had taken the money, nobody will kill somebody for such a paltry sum. Lastly, we must remember that when the accused was caught by the public, he made no mention of any money taken by Jaya. He clearly stated that he was angry because the victim didn't reciprocate his love for her. Her rejection hurt his ego and he decided to kill her.'

Judge Buka looked at Karthik, who was sitting in the dock with his head down. He wondered if what the defence lawyer had said was true. He wondered if Karthik had really loved Jaya. He wondered if Jaya had really betrayed Karthik. He wondered if Karthik really regretted what he had done. He wondered if Karthik deserved mercy and compassion.

Over the course of the next hearings, several more witnesses—bystanders, acquaintances of both the accused and the victim, etc.—were examined in the court.

Most of them repeated the same story. That they had seen the accused struggling with the victim and then slashing her throat before trying to take his own life. Mr Pantham was able to prove that none of them knew whether the knife belonged to the victim or the accused. By the time they noticed that something was wrong, the knife was already in the accused's hands. But it was possible that the victim had whipped out the knife first.

Candle in the Wind

The prosecutor also produced his own witnesses. The victim's college friends testified that Karthik had had an affair with Jaya. They also said that Karthik and Jaya were still together when she graduated and left college. Jaya's best friend Mallika claimed that Jaya was unhappy in the relationship, but the prosecutor could provide no evidence of the same.

Judge Buka raised an eyebrow and, leaning forward, said, 'Alright, it's time for the accused, Karthik Reddy, to testify. Please take the stand.'

Karthik nervously fidgeted with his fingers. 'U-uh, well, Your Honour, I-I, um, I want to say that I-I didn't do it. I was, you know, I swear, I didn't... I didn't have an-any interest in Jaya Bachu. Sh- she took my aunt's money and, um, ran away. I, uh, followed her, but, um, only to get the money back, Your Honour.'

Judge Buka squinted sceptically. He turned to look at the defence lawyer. It was evident that Judge Buka had guessed that Karthik was just parroting the lines taught to him by Gangadhar Pantham. 'I see. Please go on.'

Karthik stuttered, 'T-that's all, Your Honour.'

The prosecutor, Mr Bhaskar Kumar, crossed his arms and, leaning towards Karthik, asked, 'So, you're claiming that you had no love intentions towards her?'

Karthik nodded rapidly. 'Y-yes, exactly! And, um, at the Gandipet MeeSeva Centre, she, uh, she came at me with a knife. I, uh, I had to, um, defend myself, so I, uh, took the knife from her.' Karthik turned towards the judge and said pitifully, 'It, um, it...was an accident, Your Honour.'

The prosecutor disbelievingly raised an eyebrow. 'Go on,' he said.

In a quivering voice, Karthik said, 'A-and then, um, I realized I hurt her...bad. I-I felt so, um, guilty...*so* guilty that, uh, I wanted to, you know, end it all. That's why I turned the knife on myself.'

Mr Kumar now pounced. 'But you confessed when you were first arrested that you loved the girl and that you tried to commit suicide because you couldn't live without her.'

Karthik wiped the sweat from his brow. He said, 'Oh, th-that? Well, you see, I wasn't...thinking straight, Your Honour. I, uh, thought if I...I made up a story, it, um, it would make me look less, uh, guilty. I wasn't, um, thinking logically, like, at all.'

The prosecutor laughed. 'You should be a writer. It's quite a tale you're telling, Karthik.'

Karthik Reddy turned to the judge and said frantically, 'N-no, Your Honour, it's, uh, it's the truth! I'm not...not lying, I swear!'

Mr Kumar smirked. 'Your Honour, it's clear as day, this is just an attempt by the accused to save his own skin.'

Karthik Reddy looked visibly distressed. 'B-but, Your Honour, I-I'm telling the truth!' There was real desperation in his eyes. Even Karthik's defence lawyer was really impressed by his acting skills.

Judge Buka said firmly, 'Given the volume of material and the strain on all present, this court will adjourn for the day. The court will take a recess until tomorrow morning.'

Whispers filled the air as tension mounted in the

courtroom. Most thought that Karthik had been lying through his teeth in a desperate attempt to save himself from a harsh sentence.

※

The courtroom was in order before Judge Buka took his chair and asked for the proceedings to resume.

The prosecutor decided to produce his last and most powerful witness—Jaya's mother, Sumathi, for maximum impact.

After Sumathi had confirmed that she was the victim's mother, the prosecutor asked her gently, 'Can you tell us what happened to Jaya and what her relationship was with the accused?'

Sumathi looked broken. 'Jaya was a very good girl, Your Honour,' she said. 'Very gentle. All this talk of her stealing money breaks my heart. She was no thief. She was a good girl, who did well in her studies and was now trying to eke out a living.' She started to weep. There were murmurs of sympathy from the public who had gathered to witness the trial.

'Objection, Your Honour!' Mr Pantham said. 'The records already prove that she had stolen ₹10,000. We have submitted the evidence.'

'Objection sustained. Please continue, Mrs Sumathi.'

'Yes, Your Honour.' Sumathi took a deep gasping breath and wiped her eyes. Then she continued: 'I admit that he became Jaya's boyfriend when they met in college in Adilabad.

As it was too far away from our home in Hyderabad, she used to stay in the college hostel. Later, when she got the job with Karthik's aunt, she continued to stay in Adilabad in a women's hostel. He had relentlessly pursued her for six months when she was in college, before she submitted to his advances. But within the next six months, he started to abuse her. Still, she tried to adjust to his ways. But within a few months of her taking up the job, Karthik became more abusive and even hit her. That's when she broke up with him. She quit the job to avoid meeting him. But he wouldn't leave her alone. He continued to stalk her. When she came back home to Hyderabad, which is about two hours from his aunt's MeeSeva Centre, he followed her. We caught him trying to peep into our house. My son thrashed him and made him write a letter promising never to harass my Jaya again.'

The prosecutor stopped Sumathi. 'Here is the letter, Your Honour.' He proceeded to take out a letter, which he handed over to the court clerk, who in turn handed it to the judge, who read it with interest.

Mr Kumar, the prosecutor, turned to Sumathi and asked, 'What happened then?'

'We thought that the matter was over. So, when Jaya got a new job at the MeeSeva Centre in Gandipet, we were all very happy for her. But that horrible boy found out about her new job and followed her there. He threatened her, trying to force her to again accept him as her boyfriend. When she refused, he slit her throat. Jaya has never carried any knives with her and she has never stolen any money. I didn't bring her up like that, and I don't care what proof the defence provides; I know that she never *ever* stole any money.'

'Objection, Your Honour,' Mr Pantham shouted. 'Why does Mrs Sumathi keep denying the theft when we have provided irrefutable proof?'

'Objection sustained.' Judge Buka looked at Sumathi and said gently, 'Continue, ma'am. You don't need to focus on the theft. Just continue with your statement.'

'Yes, Your Honour. On the day that my daughter died, I was going about my morning routine as usual. A call came from the owner of the MeeSeva Centre in Gandipet. He told me that a man had attacked Jaya with a knife and that she was in hospital. I fainted right away. My instincts told me that Karthik must have attacked Jaya. My elder son, Bharat, revived me and we rushed to the hospital. But it was too late. The doctors told us that she had been brought in dead.' Sumathi started to sob in earnest.

There was an uproar in the court. Mr Bhaskar Kumar had done an excellent job in convincing the judge and the crowd that it was Karthik who had been harassing Jaya, trying to force her into a relationship with him, and had killed her when she dared to reject his advances.

Judge Buka himself no longer had any doubts as to what had happened actually. Justice may be blind, but with his vast experience of life, the judge was not; he had no doubt who the real culprit was.

Concluding Statement by the Prosecutor, Mr Bhaskar Kumar

Your Honour,
We meet today in this courtroom to discuss not only a heinous crime but also a widespread problem that affects women in society. We want the accused to pay for his action but we also want to draw attention to other problems in the system and society that lead to such tragedies.

A tragic event took place in the city of Hyderabad in India. This is a typical case of feminism in our society. A woman has been killed by a man for the crime of refusing to accept his marriage proposal. It is clear proof of the existing culture of gender-based violence.

In this court, there is a necessity to recognize the reality of gender oppression, subjugation, and violence, for the simple reason that women have the right to make their own decisions about their lives. Through centuries, our culture has perpetuated several norms and values that reinforce the gendered roles of men and women as superiors and subordinates, respectively. It is a social organization that hangs women, humiliates them and kills them for taking the liberty of choosing their life partners. We need to severely punish these men so that the punishment acts as a deterrent.

It is high time people became gender-sensitive and stopped these practices from recurring. The community and the nation have a duty to fight beliefs that lead to the oppression of women—and make women's lives free from fear. We can't allow yet another innocent person to be killed and for their death to be forgotten.

The prosecution has very good evidence which points to the guilt of the accused in this heinous crime. The accused acted with arrogance, anger and the knowledge that he could tell the victim how she should live. The victim should not have been killed for failing to comply with the perpetrator's demands. What was her crime? She simply wanted to do as she pleased. According to the accused, for that crime she had to die. It is important to remember that women's liberation is not a threat to society; it is an advantage. Women are not just possessions that men can own and control; they are equal partners in this society that is being created. If we do not punish such crimes, we are confirming to women that they should remain silent and that they have no rights. We have to break this cycle of violence and oppression, Your Honour. Please be our voice and give us a verdict that will show that violence against women is inacceptable in any form. Your Honour, the jury, it is within our power to end the victimization, to rewrite the script, and to build a world in which no woman has to live in fear or be discriminated against. The victim in this case needs justice, the victim's family needs justice and closure, and women everywhere need the justice system and society to defend their rights and lives. I ask for death penalty for the accused.

Thank you, Your Honour.

Concluding Statement by the Defence, Mr Gangadhar Pantham

Your Honour,

As we draw closer to the end of the trial, I represent the accused and submit that there was no intent on his part to kill the victim. It is my aim to introduce you to certain facts of the incident and to confront the prejudice that is still active in our society—a prejudice that quickly assigns the blame to men in cases of sexual harassment.

The accused, Mr Karthik, did not come to meet the victim with the intention of putting an end to the life of another person. He loved Jaya. Jaya didn't want to have any contact with him, and he respected that decision. But he wanted to recover the money that she had stolen from his aunt's MeeSeva Centre. This context of why he felt compelled to meet Jaya is important to highlight.

Out of the desire to get his money back, the accused engaged the victim in conversation. However, this led to a rather unforeseen confrontation—a heated argument that culminated in an accident. It was not an incident of violence that Karthik planned to commit in a cold-blooded manner. It was just an accident that happened at the spur of the moment.

The defence understands and shares the pain of the victim's family and the suffering that they have gone through.

However, we cannot and should not allow our sympathy to prejudice the proper deliberations of the facts of this case.

Honourable Judge, I request that you and the jury base your decision on pure justice and not on prejudice. Please examine all the evidence and pass your verdict based on the highest standard of proof that can be applied in a court of law—proof beyond a reasonable doubt.

༺ༀ༻

Day of Judgement: 3 January 2022

People milled about outside the courtroom. Those who came early, had long taken up the empty chairs in the room; the latecomers were left loitering outside. Media personnel, with their cameras, were gathered in a small group just outside the courtroom, waiting for the action to start. Photography was not allowed within the precincts of the courtroom. Mr Bhaskar Kumar, with his legal aids, was the first to arrive. The noise of camera shutters could be heard as soon as the media saw him. After posing for a few photographs, Mr Kumar and his team somehow made their way through the crowd into the courtroom. At the stroke of 11.00 a.m., the court clerk announced that Judge Buka had arrived, and everyone stood up. Judge Buka took his seat and began with an appreciation round, thanking everyone for their time, patience and effort in the case. He said that he had deliberated impartially and extensively, and that the court had reached a conclusion.

'At this time, please rise for the verdict,' the court clerk said.

Mr Karthik stood up along with the advocates and the police officer accompanying him. The prosecution advocates stood up, too.

Judge Buka began, 'Based on the evidence and the witness testimonies, this court finds the accused "guilty". The accused has presented that his parents are suffering from ill health and has requested a reduction in the sentence of imprisonment. Having considered the age and socio-economic background of the accused, and as there is no proof regarding past criminal antecedents, the court is of the opinion that the act of the accused does not come under the umbrella of rarest of rare cases. As such, the request of the prosecution to impose death penalty is hereby rejected and sentencing him to imprisonment for life would meet the ends of justice.

'The accused is found guilty for the offence punishable under Section 302 IPC, and the accused is convicted under Section 235 (2) CrPC, and he is sentenced to undergo imprisonment for life and also directed to pay a fine of ₹5,000. In default, he must undergo simple imprisonment for three months.

'This case is now closed. Thank you all. Jai Hind.'

There was pin-drop silence in the courtroom. Judge Buka scribbled some notes on the papers before him, signed a few documents, and then abruptly stood up, slid out from behind the desk and exited the courtroom.

Karthik's mother burst into tears. On the other side of the aisle, tears flowed down Jaya's mother's cheeks too, but in her case, they were tears of joy. While she knew she could never get her daughter back, it gave her solace to know that justice had been served.

Excerpt from Karthik's Personal Diary

When I first laid eyes on you, you were comfortably seated in a corner of the bustling students' canteen, surrounded by a close-knit group of friends. Your laughter filled the air, a beautiful symphony of joy. Your eyes sparkled with amusement, and a genuine, hearty laugh forced you to wipe away the tears of mirth that had formed in your beautiful eyes. Those eyes instantly reminded me of Sridevi.

I collected my breakfast from the counter and sat at a table next to yours, shamelessly eavesdropping on your conversation with your friends. I ate the same breakfast every day, two idlis and one vada with a cup of coffee. I am a man of routine. I hardly ever change anything, even something as mundane as the breakfast menu.

You talked breathlessly to your friends about Allu Arjun. It was evident that you had a huge crush on him, and frankly speaking, I was envious. I also came to know from your conversation that you were in first-year BCom, a year junior to me.

You chatted and giggled with your friends, your long lustrous hair tied in a ponytail with a jasmine *gajra* pinned

Unrequited Love

on it. The scent of the jasmine wafted towards me. From that time, whenever I smell jasmine, I think of you. An adorable innocent girl just burgeoning into womanhood.

I still remember the green salwar that you wore on that day, along with jhumkas studded with green stones. A green bindi adorned your fair forehead, and as for your lips... Those lips needed no lipstick as they were naturally pink. Pearly white teeth peeked out as you giggled with your friends about Allu Arjun. That day, I decided to grow a beard like Allu to impress you.

Your luxurious hair, fair skin and tall, slim build made you stand out among your friends. The others were too brash, too obvious in their tight jeans and too-tight shirts. There were other girls in my class too, who were interested in me. Particularly when they heard that I had a rich aunt with whom I was close. But they were unexciting. They were not like you.

The following week, I saw you again in the canteen. My beard had grown a little, but was yet to become a thick mane like Allu Arjun's in *Pushpa*. I wanted to whisper in your ears, '*Nenu agni, puvvu kaadu*, I am fire, not a flower.' The second time around, you were wearing a pale pink lehenga choli. The choli was cut a little too deep. I could almost imagine your perky breasts underneath the choli. I wondered if you realized that you were tantalizing the entire male population in the college. If you did, I wondered why it did not bother you. Did you take pleasure in teasing and tantalizing them? You certainly enticed me.

This time around, the conversation in your friend circle

moved from college work to relationships and boys in the college. You need a man like me, not those boys, I thought contemptuously. I hoped that one day I would be able to make you realize how superior I was to all of them. I steeled myself to listen to you discuss your boyfriend, yet my intuition proved true—all I heard was light-hearted banter about your friends' boyfriends. You had no boyfriend...*yet*. You were not like them. You were a virgin waiting for the romance of your life—a sophisticated man like me. Your own Pushpa.

I thought about you that entire week. I tried to find you between classes. I paced the college grounds, hoping to bump into you. I saw one of your friends—the tall one with the pimples—and I walked behind her for a while. But she disappeared into a teacher's room and I had to stop following her.

The next day, I made it a point to arrive early at the canteen. To my delight, there you were, sitting alone at the usual table, just as you had done on the two previous occasions. On that particular day, you seemed rather downcast and teary-eyed; strangely, it only accentuated your beauty. With my regular breakfast of idlis and vada in hand, I approached your table.

'May I sit here?'

You composed your face into the semblance of a smile and said, 'Go ahead.'

'We have seen each other before, I think,' I said, sitting opposite you.

'Really? I'm sorry, I don't remember.'

I was hurt to see that while I was obsessed over you, you hadn't even noticed me.

'I am in BCom, third year.'

'Really?' Your eyes lit up. 'Maybe you can give me your notes for the third year?'

My notes! I was an indifferent student at best, and what little notes I took would not be of use to anyone. But I had a friend who was studious and took beautiful notes. I could easily get those notes for you and pass them off as mine.

'No problem. I don't usually share my notes with anybody, but for you, I'll make an exception,' I said, looking deep into your eyes.

You didn't say anything, but two spots of colour appeared high on your cheeks and you couldn't stop the smile from spreading on your face.

'By the way, my name is Karthik Reddy.'

'Jaya Bachu,' you said shyly.

I leaned forward, 'Can I get you a coffee?'

'I like lemon tea,' you murmured, still shy.

I got up to get a coffee for myself and a lemon tea for you from the counter. When I came back, I saw your friends had arrived and taken my seat. You didn't even notice me as I walked up. Maybe you were distracted by the arrival of your friends. When I handed your cup to you, you thanked me for the lemon tea and introduced me to your friends, whose names I instantly forgot.

One of your friends asked me a question, but I couldn't take my eyes off you. A boy had also joined the group. He was talking to you earnestly, and I could see that he was attracted to you.

A strand of hair fell across your face, and you tucked it impatiently behind your ear. The aroma of jasmine from the gajra drifted to my nose. You must have felt my eyes on you, because you turned towards me and your smile was apologetic. I at once forgave your friends for intruding on our intimate—almost sacred—conversation. I stood up to leave and waited until you noticed me.

'Thank you for the lemon tea,' you said. I wanted to ask if we could see each other again, but how could I, with all your friends around you? I dragged myself away, the sound of your laughter ringing in my ears.

For the next few days, I purposely avoided any contact with you. When four days had passed, I visited the canteen again in the morning, and the perceptible sense of relief on your face assured me that my decision to stay away had been correct. This time, I didn't make any requests to join you, but instead, directly brought a cup of coffee and a lemon tea, knowing your preference.

You exclaimed, 'You remembered that I like lemon tea!'

I responded with a nonchalant shrug, as if it was a trivial matter for me.

On this occasion, I made a conscious effort to enquire more about you, being genuinely interested in learning about your life. As our conversation unfolded, I witnessed a beautiful transformation—you opened up to me like a flower gently unfurling in the morning sun. I learned that your father had passed away recently. I discerned how much

Unrequited Love

you loved him from the way your lips trembled when you spoke about him. I also learned that you had an elder brother who was a year older than me. He was a medical representative.

Soon, we were hanging out together, going for movies along with your group of friends. Everybody realized that you had a new boyfriend, and you blushed furiously whenever they teased you about us.

A month later, I invited you alone for the latest Salman Khan movie. You accepted. I found the movie rowdy and tasteless, but you seemed to enjoy it thoroughly. I forgave you your lack of taste. In time, I could teach you better taste.

'I like Salman Khan,' you declared.

But didn't you like Allu Arjun before? I wanted to ask. Are you that fickle? Will you fall out of love with me too, just like that?

After the movie we went to McDonald's. You ordered French fries and a chicken burger with soda, with no regard for the bill that I would have to pay.

'It's rare to find a woman who doesn't care about putting on weight,' I smiled, hiding my shock at your appetite behind humour.

'I am never on a diet,' you said. 'Life is too short.'

How prophetic your words would turn out to be!

But my little jibe had its effect, for you ate only half the fries and left the soda almost untouched.

'I think we should skip dessert,' I said. 'We have already had too much unhealthy food.'

I saw the disappointment on your face, but you didn't

need a fat-laden brownie sundae. Anyway, I didn't have so much money to spare.

That day, we talked about my aunt. I let it slip that she was extremely rich and owned a MeeSeva Centre. It seemed to impress you like I hoped it would. I told you that I stayed with my aunt as the college was close to her place. I explained that my parents lived in Kollur and hinted that they were rich farmers who owned a lot of land. That was not true, but a little harmless lie never hurt anybody.

You spoke about your father and how much you missed him. I learned that you stayed in a girls' hostel near the college. I dropped you there on my bike (technically, it was my cousin's bike, which I had borrowed without his knowledge). I brushed my lips against your cheeks before leaving. You blushed furiously, but seemed pleased nonetheless.

For the next few months, we were inseparable. We went to parks and restaurants. You often paid for the tickets or the restaurant bills. It was as if you realized in some corner of your mind that it would make me happy and you went out of your way to please me. After all, as you confessed to me oh so shyly, I was your first boyfriend. I told you with a roughish smile, 'Your first and only boyfriend.'

You were mine. If I couldn't have you, then nobody else would either.

Then one weekend, my aunt and her family went to Tirupati for two days. I was left in charge. I brought you back to the house. As soon as we were inside the house, I started to kiss you. You kissed me back, and I felt your tongue exploring my mouth, while your hands ran over my back and shoulders. With a gentle nudge, I guided you towards my bed.

You hesitated. 'Slow down,' you requested, though your smile betrayed your true feelings.

'I can't,' I confessed. 'You're gorgeous, and I can't restrain myself.'

A pink flush appeared across your face as you tried to speak, but I didn't let you.

'Hush,' I whispered, leaning in to kiss you again. 'You are the loveliest thing, Jaya. You turn me on so much.'

You responded with another kiss, abandoning pretences. It was evident that you wanted it just as bad as I did.

We made love. As I had guessed, you were a virgin. After we made love, you whispered in my ears, 'Promise me, you will never leave me!' I promised.

You said that you would prepare lunch for me. You carefully prepared sambar after calling your mom for instructions. It didn't taste too bad. But I don't know what made me spoil it all for you. I took one spoon of the rice and sambar that you had prepared with so much love, and made a face.

'What?' You asked anxiously.

'It's okay-okay,' I said and pushed my plate away from me. I got up from the table with most of the rice uneaten. 'I'm not hungry.'

Your face fell, and I felt instantly better as though I had picked off the scaly flakes from an old dried sore.

'I'm sorry,' I said. 'You went to so much trouble just for me.'

Candle in the Wind

'No, it's fine,' you said. But it was clear that you were offended. I thought you would spend the rest of the day sulking, but you seemed cheerful enough after watching one of the cheap Telugu serials you seemed to enjoy so much. That evening, I took you out for dinner at Ram ki Bandi. You ate heartily. Two dosas! But I forgave you. You must have been hungry as you had eaten next to nothing for lunch.

I deliberately kept away from you on Sunday. Instead, I met up with my friends and boasted about my new conquest—*you*. I embellished a bit, I must admit. I boasted about your prowess in bed, when you had been insipid at best. I made them promise not to tell anyone, but by Tuesday the news had spread like wildfire. Your friends came to know and told you. Of course, I denied everything when you confronted me about it. But you knew that I was lying.

'I want to marry you, Jaya. Why would I tell them about us?' I pleaded.

But you were determined to break off the relationship. It took a great deal of cajoling before I could finally convince you to give our relationship another chance. But something in your attitude towards me had changed. You were more wary of me. More measured when talking to me. And you refused to sleep with me again. 'After marriage,' you would say, pretending to be shy. But I knew that you were being cautious. Soon, I graduated and left college. But I continued to stay with my aunt and pretended to study for MBA entrance exams. You were in third year now and doing quite well in studies. We were looking forward to your bright future. During that time, we had had our ups and downs, but I always knew how to get my way, how to make you accept my apologies. You too quickly learned to apologize for any of your transgressions that I pointed out. I knew how to make you do as I asked. You were a bright student. Very soon you learned how to keep me happy. I knew that I had made you mine and only mine, in body and mind. After graduation, you didn't want to study further. You wanted to get a job. I liked your fiercely independent spirit. Also, once you had a job, you would be able to spend more money on me.

I got you a job at my aunt's MeeSeva Centre. But when I proposed marriage, you said, 'Karthik, right now you don't have a job.'

'Arrey, I'm studying for my MBA entrance. Once I become an MBA, I will earn a lot of money,' I said.

But you wouldn't agree to the marriage. I began to worry that you were falling out of love with me. Maybe you had found someone else. Maybe it was that boy who frequented the MeeSeva Centre on some pretext or the other.

One day, I caught the two of you chatting and laughing. That day, when we met at the park—as was our usual custom—I was in an ugly mood. All I had thought about throughout the day was the way you had simpered, the way you had blushed and let that ugly man in the MeeSeva Centre flirt with you. How you had *enjoyed* it. As we entered the park at 3.30 p.m. you chattered lightly, *cheerfully*, as if nothing was wrong. The bubble of pressure that had been building inside me since I saw you laughing with that yob in the MeeSeva Centre, was growing with your inane chatter. It was pushing my lungs apart, making it difficult for me to breathe. My eyelids were twitching and my head was heavy with rage. I looked around. At this time, the park was empty. The children were yet to come with their mothers. The day was hot and no other couple was loitering nearby. As soon as we sat on our usual bench on the park, I raised my fist and slammed it in your face. Almost immediately, the bubble of anger burst and calm washed over me. My headache eased and my eyelids ceased to twitch. A strangled gurgle emanated from your throat and blood spurted from your nose. It was the most beautiful thing I had ever seen.

I walked away from the park, feeling a lot lighter. The next day, you didn't report to work. My aunt asked me why you hadn't come. I guessed you were still nursing your broken nose. I didn't call you immediately, wanting things to calm down a bit before coaxing and cajoling you to forgive me. I knew you would forgive me. You always did. But when you didn't show up for work again the next day, I got worried.

When I enquired at your hostel, they said you had packed your bags and left. Had you run off with that yob you were flirting with? Had he told you he would give you anything that you wanted? And what had you offered in return? You disgusted me. I told myself I was better off without you. But I still couldn't stop myself from searching for you. I roamed the streets on my cousin's bike searching for you every day. Till one day, I found you. I caught sight of

Unrequited Love

you as you got off the bus and walked into Pringle Hospital. I sent a friend of mine to check what you were doing at the hospital. He reported that you had a job there as a receptionist.

The next morning, at 10.00 a.m., I strolled into the hospital. Your face went white when you saw me. But you didn't want to create a scene, so you agreed to meet me outside. When I asked you to stop running from me and marry me, you flatly refused. You told me point blank that in the year and half that you had known me, you didn't spend a single happy day and that I had abused you constantly. I was flabbergasted. Nobody could love you more than me. I tried to explain to you that I was obsessed with you and that I couldn't possibly live without you. Even then, you weren't convinced and repeatedly asked me to leave you alone. Finally, you started to cry and the people on the road must have thought that I was abusing you. It was then that I lost my temper and called you a slut and slapped you. The security guards came out running and a crowd began to gather, forcing me to leave.

The next day, when I returned to the hospital, you had vanished. I searched for you everywhere, but I couldn't find you. I realized that there was only one place you would run to—your mother's place. When you applied for employment at my aunt's MeeSeva Centre, you had written down your permanent address as your mother's place in Secunderabad.

I had no trouble locating the modest single-storeyed home in Begumpet where you stayed with your mother and brother. I tried to peep in through a half-closed window in the hope of catching a glimpse of you. Unfortunately, a nosy, well-muscled neighbour noticed what I was doing and raised an alarm. I tried to run away but was caught by the man, and soon, you arrived on the scene with your mother and brother to see what the commotion was all about. Your eyes widened in shock and fear as soon as you realized that I had found you. I had hoped that I would see love in your eyes, but there was no trace of it.

I was thrashed by your brother and some of his well-muscled friends. Then, they made me write a letter promising never to follow or harass you. I didn't want to write the letter, but they had beaten me black and blue and I was bleeding. I saw no empathy in those beautiful, cruel eyes of yours. You could have felt a little sad for me, could you not? After all, we had been lovers. You even cooked food for me.

After I had reluctantly written the letter, they let me go. I went back to my aunt's house. You know, at the time I really thought I would let you go. But you kept invading my dreams. I wanted you so bad, it hurt. There was no way I could stay away from you. I cried in my sleep, taking your name. I was obsessed with you. Then, I heard that you had taken up a job in a new MeeSeva Centre in Gandipet. They had called my aunt to check that you had really worked for us. I looked up the address of the Gandipet MeeSeva Centre on the internet, and travelled there the next day. There was a tea stall right outside the MeeSeva Centre from where I had a view of your desk inside. I watched you all day as you dealt with customers. There was another young man who was working at the desk right next to you. I later came to know that he was the owner's son. He seemed to be smitten by you and kept stealing glances at you. You too seemed to be attracted to him. You went out for lunch with him at a nearby Udupi restaurant. I saw him deliberately brush against you, but you didn't seem to be offended.

Jaya...Jaya...how could you forget me so easily? Why did you abandon me? You once extracted a promise from me that I would never ever leave you. I am a man of my word. I will never leave you. And I won't let you leave me either.

I went back to my aunt's place and collected a sharp knife.

The next morning, I returned to Gandipet. I saw the owner of the MeeSeva Centre and his son open the Centre at 10.00 a.m. sharp. They fiddled around with the computers. I know enough about MeeSevas to understand that they were booting up the systems. Then, at 10.30 a.m. sharp, you walked in. You were looking beautiful as usual in a white salwar suit. I walked into the MeeSeva Centre. You paled as soon as you saw me. Your reaction irritated me. Is this the way to reciprocate my love for you?

'I want to speak to you,' I said.

The young man, your new *boyfriend*, objected. But you looked at him pleadingly, silently asking him not to create a scene. You were always afraid of scenes. You told him, 'I know him. I will just go outside, speak to him and come back in five minutes.'

The young man nodded reluctantly.

You came out with me. 'Why are you here, Karthik?' You asked sharply. 'Why can't you leave me alone!'

'Because I love you and if you can't be mine, you can never be anybody else's,' I said, grinding my teeth like a mad man.

'Get *lost*!'

Your contempt was evident as you turned to go back into the office.

On the way to Gandipet, I was not sure if I should kill you. But your utter contempt for me left room for no doubt in my mind. You had to die. And I had to die with you. We would be united in death, if not in life. I grabbed you by your long hair, the hair that had attracted me to you in the first place. Then I took out the knife from my pocket and slashed your throat three times.

The young man had been watching us from his desk. He started shouting. He and his father rushed towards us. By this time, you had fallen to the ground, bleeding profusely. I looked at you approvingly. Finally you had found your rightful place. At my feet.

I took the knife and tried to slash my own throat. But by this time, a few more people from the nearby tea stall had rushed towards us. They prevented me from slashing my own throat. Not that I needed much persuasion. I am sorry, Jaya, but when the time came for me to join you, my courage failed. I was shouting like a madman that I loved you and that I wanted to kill you and myself. They thrashed me and tied me to a tree. A constable who was passing by noticed the commotion and came running towards us. He called his seniors as soon as he realized what was happening. I was taken to the Gandipet Police Station, where I confessed to the murder, but I said that I didn't mean to kill you; it was an accident. Which was true in a way. After all, I wouldn't have killed you if you had accepted me as your lover. Then I was sent to Chanchalguda Jail. I was denied bail by the judge, who said that I had committed a 'heinous crime'.

It's all your fault, Jaya. Why did you anger me so much by running away from me? We could have gotten married and led a wonderful life together. You ruined it all.

In the Name of the Children

11 August 2020

Dear God,

Yesterday, I overheard the nurse in the hospital say that I am going to meet you soon. But you know what? I don't want to meet you. After all, I am only fourteen. Why do you want to meet me so early?

They say those who are loved by God die young. But do you really love me? I don't think so. If you truly love me, why did you take away my mother when I was only nine? Why did my father drown himself in alcohol, abandoning me to this desolate existence? Why, oh why, was I cast away to wither within the cold, loveless walls of an orphanage?

They say that you are just. They say that you are kind. But I don't think so. I think that you are cruel and heartless. For, if you cared even a shred, you would never have allowed all this suffering to befall me, would you?

I hate you, do you understand? I hate you!

Why am I even writing to you? There is no point, is there?

Harshita.

In the Name of the Children

15 September 2020, 9.00 a.m.

Divya, a scrawny fourteen-year-old girl, stands before the tiny basin in one corner of the tiny kitchen of a tiny one-bedroom house. She is wearing a faded salwar-kameez that is too big for her, a hand-me-down from her seventeen-year-old cousin Priya.

The house belongs to her aunt, Mira chachi, her late father's sister. Her uncle, aunt and their three bratty children don't want her around. Two years ago, they had admitted her to an orphanage after her parents had died. But they have been forced to take her in again, as the orphanage was closed due to COVID-19 restrictions.

Mira chachi is a good cook, and she is making puri-bhaji for breakfast. The aroma of frying puris makes Divya's mouth water. She's so hungry that her stomach hurts. She hopes Mira chachi will give her some breakfast. Her last meal was at lunchtime the day before, almost twenty hours back, and had consisted only of sambar and some leftover rice from the previous night.

Divya's eyes are puffy from crying and her body hurts all over. Last night, Mira chachi had beaten her up because a hundred rupees was missing from her purse. Divya knew that it was her seventeen-year-old cousin Varun, a high-school dropout, who had taken the money. But if she had snitched on him, the retribution from Varun would have been

Candle in the Wind

even worse. So, she had taken the beating in silence and been sent off to bed without dinner. Her bed was no more than a bedsheet and a dirty pillow on the floor. Curled up on the floor, she had cried herself to sleep, wishing bitterly that the orphanage would reopen so that she could go back there. She had been better off at the orphanage.

Right now, she is washing utensils as her aunt continues to fry puris. Her uncle's phone rings. Divya's ears perk up as she tries to listen to what is being said. She knows she's being nosy, but all the hardships she has faced in her life have not been able to stamp out the inherent curiosity she has about other people. To her surprise, the call is about Harshita. Divya's curiosity fires up even more when she realizes that the call is from the police and that they want to talk to her about Harshita.

Can this be about that man who used to take Harshita to the fifth-floor room of the orphanage where other children were not allowed to go? She remembers how Harshita used to suffer from severe pain in her abdomen after the man left. Had Harshita finally gained enough courage to complain against that man?

And then, Divya's heart almost stops.

'Dead?' Her uncle is saying to the police. 'You say the girl is dead?'

༄

Nandini is working in the fields with her stepmother, Durga. Her stepbrother, Tejas, is away at school. He goes to an English-medium school in the nearby town and stays in the school hostel. His mother has big dreams for him and is determined that he will never be a small-time farmer like his father, Raghu. Most of the money that Nandini's father earns is spent on Tejas's education.

When Nandini was eight years old, her mother died. Durga had agreed to marry Nandini's father on the condition that Nandini would never stay with them. So, Raghu had admitted Nandini into the orphanage before he married Durga. When Anisha, the manager of the Sridevi Orphanage, had called Raghu, asking him to take Nandini home as the orphanage was closing due to COVID-19, Durga had been livid and thrown a huge tantrum. Raghu, ever-grateful that Durga had agreed to marry a much older man like him and had given him a son, promised to pack off Nandini back to the orphanage as soon as possible.

Meanwhile, Durga ensures that Nandini earns her keep by making her work in the fields. She also has to help with washing the clothes and utensils.

'I wish you had died along with your mother,' her father mutters, when Nandini tries to protest against the back-breaking grind that her stepmother puts her through. Her stepmother slaps her and makes her work even harder.

A few days later, Raghu receives a call from the police. For a minute, he is frightened. Has some neighbour complained about the way he and Durga treat Nandini? To his relief, the call is about something else altogether.

Hanging up, he tells Nandini, 'One of your roommates

in the orphanage has died. I'll need to take you to the police station.'

Her stepmother mutters, 'I wish it was you who had died instead. But God has not blessed me with such kind of luck.' She glares at Raghu and says, 'Instead, I am saddled with a *buddha* like your father. And you!'

Nandini bursts into tears. Not because of the harsh way in which her father and stepmother treat her—she is used to such cruelty by now. But Harshita? Harshita was her roommate and best friend in the orphanage; one of the very few people who had ever loved her. She used to help Nandini with her studies and was one of the loveliest girls she had ever known. And now, she is dead.

She knew that something bad was happening to Harshita when all the girls in the orphanage were told to leave due to COVID-19, but Harshita wasn't allowed to leave even though she had been so sick. Nandini is sure that the man who used to take Harshita to the fifth-floor room has something to do with her death. She remembers how Harshita had started to lose bladder control after the first few times the man took her up to that fifth-floor room. How she used to be in terrible pain all the time.

She wishes she had been courageous enough to tell some grown-up about what was happening to Harshita. But who would have believed her?

Urmila is presently staying with her sister Lavanya, who is married to a rich man who can easily afford to feed one extra mouth. But Lavanya's mother-in-law, Hema, is a mean woman.

'My foolish son married you without taking a single paisa in dowry. You should be grateful that we allow you to stay here. Don't expect us to feed your sister, too. We are not running a charity here.'

'Not running a charity here.' That's the constant refrain Lavanya has heard since the day she got married to Hema's son, Rakesh, five years back. All these years later, she has still not got used to Hema's insults. Lavanya is too thin-skinned. If girls from poor families have such thin skins, they invariably suffer. Unfortunately, Urmila too is like Lavanya.

Lavanya is very scared of Hema. She is treated like an unpaid servant in the family. Her husband, Rakesh, who had fallen in love with her at first sight when she came to work as a nurse for his sick father, does his best to protect her. But he is no match for his sadistic mother who takes great pleasure in insulting and, occasionally, even beating Lavanya. When Urmila and Lavanya's parents died in a freak accident, Lavanya had broached the subject of keeping her then six-year-old sister, Urmila, with them. But Hema had bluntly refused.

'We are taking care of you. Now you want us to feed another mouth! What do you think? Have we opened a charity here? Rakesh, you fool, why did you have to marry into such a poor family! We could have got so much money in dowry!' Even after five years, Hema can't forgive her son for being foolish enough to marry into a poor family where the bride's parents couldn't pay any dowry.

Rakesh had tried to reason with his mother. 'Where will her sister go? Please be reasonable.'

But Hema had put her foot down. 'We have suffered enough losses since this *ammayi* has come into our lives; she only brings bad luck. If you dare bring her good-for-nothing sister into this house, I'll leave.'

Finally, Lavanya and Rakesh were forced to admit Urmila into an orphanage. But now, Urmila has been sent back home as the orphanage has been closed due to COVID. Every day, Hema insults both the sisters and makes life hell for them. Hema ensures that Urmila is given the barest minimum in terms of food and basic necessities. But Rakesh occasionally buys cakes and sweets stealthily for Lavanya and Urmila.

Urmila prays for the orphanage to reopen soon. She particularly misses her friend Harshita and hopes she has recovered her health. Urmila had last seen Harshita when Rakesh had come to take Urmila. At that time, Harshita was still at the orphanage and was suffering from severe abdominal pain. She was so weak that she could hardly walk to the bathroom. Urmila recalls how Harshita had vomited in her bed and lost bladder control. Srinath sir, Anisha ma'am's brother, had beaten her up and ordered her to wash the soiled bedsheet even though Harshita could barely stand. Urmila had helped her in the end, else Srinath would have beaten Harshita again. Just before the closure of the orphanage, Srinath had bought some medicines for

Harshita from the nearby pharmacy. Urmila holds on to the hope that Harshita's health has improved since then.

Then, there is a call from the police to Rakesh, who is Urmila's official guardian. Some ACP wants to meet Urmila regarding the death of her friend Harshita.

∽

Divya, Nandini and Urmila are very nervous when they arrive at the Bharosa Centre, but they perk up when they see each other. They are meeting after being apart for several weeks and give each other high fives like they have seen kids do in the TV serials they were allowed to watch in the orphanage.

Nandini: 'Hiiii... Divya, hi Urmila, I was seriously missing you both. How's life? Uff, I'd rather be back at the orphanage, yaar. I just don't get this whole COVID drama. Why did we have to go home? Couldn't we just have stayed put at the orphanage? I'm telling you, life at home is a total nightmare. My stepmom gives me a good hiding every time I don't abjectly obey her.'

Urmila (with a bitter twist to her lips): 'Well, at least I'm better off, yaar. My relatives don't lay a hand on me. They simply ignore or insult me and mutter eagerly about the day I will be back at the orphanage. My poor sister is suffering so much because of me. I wish the orphanage would reopen soon so that she can get some peace.'

Divya sighs: 'Seriously, we were so much better off at the orphanage. But listen, you heard about Harshita, *na*?'

Eyes rounded in fear, she looks around to check if anybody is within earshot. Then she whispers: 'Harshita is dead!'

Nandini's face crumples as she says: 'Yes, my father told me.'

Urmila says, covering her cheeks with her hands: 'It must be because of those tablets that man used to feed her.'

Nandini: 'The police are trying to figure out what went on at the orphanage. They will question us about what really happened.'

Urmila (looking scared): 'Oh my god, should we tell the police? What if Anisha ma'am comes after us too?'

∞

12 May 2015

Ravi is drunk. His wife, Savitri, is dying back at home. But he doesn't care. After finishing one full bottle of rum, Ravi feels like he's on top of the world. He weaves his way back drunkenly to his home—a tiny single room in the basement of a dilapidated house. It is 10.30 p.m. There is no electricity. The landlord has cut off the supply as Ravi hasn't paid the rent for the last six months.

His wife is sleeping, almost comatose, on the floor in a fetal position, lines of pain etched on her face. She is suffering from cancer, but there's no money to pay for the treatment. Whatever money Ravi earns is spent on his food, alcohol and an occasional visit to the prostitute.

Their daughter sleeps beside her mother on the floor. Her hand lies outstretched on the floor in sleep, and Ravi steps on it in the darkness. The girl wakes up in pain and starts wailing.

'Shut up,' Ravi snarls, raising his hand threateningly.

The child stops crying, shrinking in fear from her own father.

The next morning, the child runs screaming to their neighbour's house and bangs on the door. She had tried to wake her mother up, but she was deep in sleep and wouldn't wake up.

The neighbour, a kind-hearted man named Samuel, opens the door.

'What happened, Harshita?' He asks, concerned.

∽

3 June 2015, Sridevi Orphanage

Samuel and Harshita are sitting in the reception area.

A fat lady, wearing a sari and sweating profusely, waddles in and sits down behind the desk.

The nameplate on the desk reads, 'Anisha, Manager'.

Samuel produces a letter from the local MLA. Anisha reads the letter and inspects Harshita from head to toe. Samuel shudders at the cold severity of the glance. The fat woman is neither kind nor smiling. But what can he do?

He has three children of his own, a total of five mouths to feed. As a lowly construction labourer, he cannot afford the burden of one more child.

Anisha is speaking.

'Why do you want to admit this child to the orphanage? Her father is still alive, no?'

Samuel responds, 'Madam, her father has left the family and can't be traced. Anyway, he's an alcoholic.' He shrugs.

A poignant silence that needs no explanation follows. Anisha glances at the letter from the MLA. She can't disregard the letter. After all, it is the same MLA who gave her the licence to open the orphanage. It's quite a lucrative business, as she spends only half the grant that the government gives on the residents and pockets the rest. Grudgingly, she says, 'Okay, I'll take her in.'

Harshita walks back home with Samuel to pack her meagre belongings.

If she sheds tears at being dislocated from her home, nobody notices. If she sheds tears that her mother is dead, nobody cares. Everybody is struggling to cope with their own problems. Who has the time for a nine-year-old almost-orphan girl child?

∞

4 January 2020

Mr Satish is a senior director in Bacchu's Laboratory, a well-known pharmaceutical company. He is a brilliant chemist and a star performer in the company—a highly professional man who is warm and charming with his colleagues. He's particularly liked by the female colleagues, as he is gentlemanly with them, given to old-school courtesies like holding doors open. Most importantly, he understands office politics well and he knows how to keep secrets. He also knows how to make his rather lazy boss totally reliant on him.

Right now, he is giving a presentation on flunitrazepam. His team has experimented with this drug and has made some chemical alterations. Now, it is being touted as a wonder drug for the treatment of insomnia. At least, that's how the management wants to market it. The senior management listens in rapt attention as Satish outlines how the drug, after the modification, can be legalized and sold over the counter. All the attendees nod their approval except for the lone voice of the director, Mr Raman.

'Isn't flunitrazepam sold illegally as a date-rape drug?' he asks.

Trust Raman to come up with an inconvenient question. Satish curses the man mentally. But he is the boss and Satish cannot ignore the query. 'Good question,' he says smoothly. 'We have been experimenting with this drug. We have changed its chemical composition sufficiently, so that we now have a drug which acts as a sleeping tablet, but without being habit-forming or damaging the brain.'

'Are you sure? Has sufficient testing been done?' Satish's boss Naveen Reddy, the head of the Hyderabad office, asks, suddenly wary. 'This might bring negative publicity for the company if it becomes publicly known.'

'Not to worry, sir,' Satish says glibly. 'My team has altered the chemical composition. We have tested it thoroughly on lab mice. No side effects at all. It's a good alternative to sleeping tablets. It'll be approved.'

'If this drug passes all the tests, millions of our customers will benefit. Satish, I hope you have patented this. If all goes well, the company will mint money. Share prices will shoot up,' Naveen Reddy says, rubbing his hands gleefully.

After the meeting, Satish starts for home. He's happy. The meeting has gone well, and he's sure he will be promoted soon. He can't wait to reach home and tell his wife all about his great achievement. He lives in a three-storeyed villa, about twenty minutes' drive from his office. Any movie star would be proud of owning such a villa. The area was desolate and underdeveloped when he had bought the property. But the land value has appreciated exponentially since then. Now the villa is worth six times the price at which he had bought it. He is a shrewd man and he knows it.

As is his usual routine, he reaches home by 7.30 p.m.

He rings the doorbell. Their live-in maid servant, Malti, a woman in her forties, quietly opens the door and stands aside, her head bowed. Satish ignores her as he discards his shoes and dons the chappals that she has kept ready. Malti bends and puts his office shoes away in the shoe rack.

Satish goes straight to Lakshmi's room, located on the ground floor. It has a magnificent view of the backyard with its large lawn, lined with mayflower and mango trees and beautifully manicured shrubs.

Lakshmi is their chirpy eleven-year-old daughter. She is very pretty. Satish protects her with all his might against this evil, evil world. He knows how evil the world can be. Lakshmi is spoilt, but eminently lovable. She lacks for nothing. Toys, love, clothes, the best education—there's nothing Satish wouldn't do for her. He thinks the world of his little princess.

He finds Lakshmi lounging on her bed, playing with her mobile.

'Finished your homework, princess?' Satish asks, pinching her cheeks lightly.

'Papa, you hurt me!' Lakshmi yells playfully.

'Come, Papa has come home. Let's eat and chat a bit,' Satish says, tickling her lightly.

'No, Papa! Don't... I'm coming,' Lakshmi giggles.

Hearing the commotion, his wife Rani comes in. Smiling, she takes his laptop bag from his hand.

'How was your day?' She asks.

'Arrey, it was excellent. I'll tell you all about it after dinner. Let me freshen up first,' Satish says. 'And you!' He wags a finger at Lakshmi, 'Better finish whatever you are doing and come to the dinner table in ten minutes.'

Rani keeps the laptop bag in Satish's home-office on the second floor. Rani and Satish have separate bedrooms on the second floor. There is also a magnificent terrace full of flowering plants. Rani is very fond of plants. She has employed two gardeners who tend to her terrace garden and backyard.

She goes down to the dining room to ensure that Malti has prepared dinner according to Satish's liking. She is pleased to see that the curries have been put in casseroles, and the dining table has been set for dinner. Malti is waiting in the kitchen to start preparing the chapatis once the family sits down to dinner. Satish likes his chapatis hot. Once Malti had been sick, so Rani had prepared the chapatis beforehand and kept them in a casserole. Satish had flown into a huge rage.

'I work so hard every day and keep you in such luxury. You can't even give me hot chapatis! Get rid of Malti if she is sick. Or get another temporary maid. But don't give me stale chapatis ever again!'

Even Lakshmi had been scared at his sudden outburst.

Later on, he had been apologetic. 'I'm sorry. I was hungry, and had had a bad day at work.'

Satish loves his wife and daughter. He treats Rani like a queen. He believes that Rani has brought him good luck, and there are no whims or demands of hers that he wouldn't gladly fulfil. He is also a good father to Lakshmi. There is nothing he would not do to protect his family. He is the perfect family man, except for the occasional outbursts of rage triggered by deviations from his wishes. He seeks compliance and expects his wife to manage the house according to his needs and comforts—a modest concession for the opulent lifestyle he has generously provided her.

He is also a religious and highly superstitious man. A man who loves routine. He is in office by 10.00 a.m. and returns by 7.30 p.m. like clockwork, and spends the evening either working or chatting with his wife and playing with his daughter.

He visits the temple every Saturday after breakfast. Recently, for about two months, he has started donating to an orphanage near the temple. He likes to take care of the little orphan girls. He is normally back before lunch. The rest of the weekend, he spends quality time with his family. Once a month, he has to visit other branches of his company, which he does uncomplainingly and unfailingly. Though he is a kind and considerate husband, he stopped sleeping with his wife almost immediately after his daughter was born.

Rani can't remember the last time they had sex.

Rani had once asked him, a few months after Lakshmi's birth, 'There's something that's been bothering me. You've been avoiding sleeping with me for a while now. Is it something I have done?'

Satish had become uncomfortable. Squirming slightly, he had said, 'No, Rani, it's not you. It's...me.'

Rani had asked in a concerned voice, 'What do you mean?'

Satish had sighed. 'I've been facing some health issues, Rani. I have erectile dysfunction.'

Rani had been surprised and worried. 'Oh, Satish, I had no idea. Why didn't you tell me sooner?'

Satish lowered his eyes, clearly embarrassed. 'I was ashamed. But I promise, I'm trying to work on it. It's just that...'

Rani had asked encouragingly, 'Just what, Satish?'

Satish said hesitantly, 'I believe visiting the temple and praying will heal me somehow.'

Rani said in a concerned voice, 'Satish! You can't be this superstitious! You should see a doctor. It could be a medical issue that needs proper treatment.'

Satish had started to become angry. 'Be patient, Rani! I'm trying to overcome it my own way.'

Rani said, 'I understand, but your well-being is important to me. We're partners in this journey, remember?'

'I don't want to discuss this anymore!' Satish had snapped angrily.

That was the first time after their marriage that Rani had witnessed Satish's rage. Rani tried to broach the topic a few more times. But every time, he had flown into a rage, and after a while, she stopped trying to discuss the matter.

Rani is a rather naïve woman. She wears her heart on her sleeve. She would have never done well in the corporate world—the world where her husband thrives. But she hates routine and finds the life she leads with her husband boring and monotonous. She feels like a caged bird, and has no idea how to escape her golden cage.

Sometimes, she cries out of sheer frustration. Her daughter, Lakshmi, runs up to her, hugs her and asks, 'Ma, why are you crying?' How can Rani explain to her little girl why she cries and howls in the privacy of her bedroom like a demented woman? To the world outside, she has everything a woman could possibly want. House, money to spend, cars, drivers, jewellery, a beautiful daughter. Yet, why is she suicidal? Rani herself cannot understand why she is so depressed.

She considers having an affair. But she is afraid. What if Satish comes to know? What if all her material comforts are taken away from her? What if Lakshmi is taken away from her? Satish is rich and powerful enough to do that. Satish may love her, but his occasional temper tantrums scare her. Rani has become so soft from her comfortable lifestyle that she dreads these rages and does everything possible to avoid such situations.

For example, one Saturday, Satish had gone to visit the temple, and returned only in the evening. Even his phone was switched off. But when Rani tried to question why he was so late, he snapped. He flew into a rage, accused her of being paranoid and not trusting him, and refused his lunch. He remained angry till the next morning. But the next morning, after breakfast, he tiptoed to his wife's bedroom asking if he could come in. He hugged her and apologized. Rani hid the fact that she had cried herself to sleep after he had shouted at her.

She is so used to him petting her and loving her like she was his favourite dog, that his temper tantrums shock her to her core. But she is smart enough to not allow Satish to see how hurt she feels. Satish can—and will—exploit her weaknesses. Also, Rani is willing to compromise her own feelings because she knows how much Satish loves Lakshmi.

Tomorrow is Lakshmi's twelfth birthday. They plan to go to the temple. Then they will go to the orphanage, where little girls the same age as Lakshmi reside. Lakshmi will hand over a large donation. Satish is very familiar with the orphanage as he regularly donates there. After the orphanage visit, they have planned a grand birthday party.

Satish has invited all his seniors and his important colleagues to the party. It will be a good opportunity to advance his chances of a promotion.

∽

When Mr and Mrs Satish reach the orphanage with Lakshmi, Anisha greets them like royalty. Lakshmi hands over a cheque—worth ₹100,000—to Anisha.

A thin, undernourished girl comes in with a tray of tea and snacks for the family.

Satish stares at the child carrying the tray. He licks his lips.

Mrs Satish pinches the child's cheeks affectionately.

'What's your name?'

'Harshita, ma'am,' the child answers hesitantly.

Anisha smiles indulgently at Harshita. 'She's a good girl. Very studious and obedient. We send all students of the orphanage to the government English-medium school nearby. She wants to become a doctor.'

'Writer, ma'am,' Harshita mumbles in a low voice.

But Anisha doesn't hear Harshita nor does she care about Harshita's dream. She's busy with her own dreams of all the things she can do with this unexpected windfall. Maybe she can put in Italian flooring for the palatial house she is building quite close to the orphanage for her own family.

∽

11 January 2020

On the following Saturday, Satish visits the orphanage again, generously donating an additional amount of ₹50,000. He had been actively seeking an opportunity to fulfil his guilty pleasure, and he has found the perfect outlet in this particular orphanage.

Over the past two months, he has made frequent visits to the orphanage after his trips to the temple. During these visits, he showed interest in the well-being of the orphan girls and contributed small amounts of money to support them. Remarkably, he never insisted on receipts for his contributions.

Through his consistent efforts and financial support, Satish has effectively built a strong rapport with the orphanage's manager, Anisha, and her brother, Srinath, who also serves as the driver. Srinath plays a significant role in the orphanage's operations, transporting the girls to and from a nearby school. Unfortunately, his behaviour towards the girls is often harsh; he sometimes resorts to physical punishment if they take too long to get ready. Besides Anisha and Srinath, the orphanage operates with very little staff, as the girls are made to shoulder the burden by laundering their own clothes and bedding, maintaining cleanliness in their rooms, cooking, and washing their dishes after meals.

Anisha and Srinath are flattered that an influential man like Satish is interested in the orphanage. He even promises a good job for Srinath in his company.

Finally, after several donations, Satish feels comfortable enough to tell Srinath what he really wants. He promises to bring several more donors to the orphanage in return. He knows that with such bribes and enticements, his secret will be safe with Anisha and Srinath. Earlier, he had to limit himself to indulging his craving only on out-of-town work trips. But now, thanks to the orphanage, he can indulge in his pleasures every week.

And the girls? They are the softest little targets. Who cares if these little buggers die? Their life has no value as far as Satish is concerned. They were born to cater to his needs. Nobody will ever know about his little escapades here. His secret is perfectly safe. Or so he thinks.

Anisha summons Harshita to her office. 'Harshita, you are so weak. You need to build up strength,' she says, caressing Harshita's hair. 'There is a doctor uncle who wants to do a checkup. He is in the fifth-floor room. Why don't you go and meet him? Do as he says, do you understand?' There is a hint of a threat in her voice. Harshita is surprised, as usually no one is allowed on the fifth floor which Anisha has reserved for her own use, but she nods obediently. Everybody is scared of Anisha ma'am and Harshita knows the consequences of disobeying her won't be pleasant.

She goes up to the fifth floor, where she finds Satish waiting. He pretends to check Harshita's pulse.

'Hmm... You have poor circulation. Have this tablet, you will feel better.' He produces a tablet and a bottle of water.

Harshita obediently gulps down the tablet. She is almost

the same age as Satish's daughter, Lakshmi. But in Satish's view, poor, parentless girls like Harshita don't count.

Harshita becomes unconscious soon after having the date-rape drug. Satish swiftly undresses himself, then undresses Harshita at a much slower pace, taking pleasure in every movement. He is a big bull of a man. If he has erectile dysfunction, there is no sign of it now. He tries to mount the little girl but she is too small for him. Impatiently, he uses a lubricant and then with great force, penetrates her little body. Then, he roughly begins to shove against her. Harshita's body convulses, and her head strikes the wall at the head of the bed. Satish doesn't notice. Even in her unconscious state, Harshita moans in pain. Satish doesn't stop. After having his fill, he leaves the unconscious girl on the bed, naked, while he dresses up and hurriedly leaves. He is afraid that his wife might suspect something if he is late again.

Divya had seen Harshita go up to the fifth floor. Curious, she waits near the stairs for Harshita to come down. Instead, she notices Satish rushing down the stairs from the fifth floor. She wonders who this man is and what he was doing on the fifth floor with Harshita. Peeping from the window of her bedroom which she shares with Harshita, Nandini and Urmila, she sees the man driving off in a hurry. She tells her roommates what she saw, and they all wonder why Harshita has not yet returned from the fifth floor. They hesitate for some time, as they know that the fifth floor is out of bounds for them. But when Harshita doesn't appear even after fifteen minutes, they finally muster up courage to go and check on her.

They are shocked to find her naked, still unconscious. There are bruises all over her body and a lot of blood on the bedsheet. They sprinkle water on her to wake her up. They dress her up. Harshita is so weak that she can barely walk. She is sore all over. Her friends help her down to their bedroom.

Harshita goes to Anisha the next day to tell her what happened.

Instead of showing any concern, Anisha slaps Harshita hard.

As Harshita stares at her in shock, Anisha says harshly, 'Why are you telling such lies? That man is a doctor and he is giving you medications to build up your strength. You should be grateful that he has chosen you for treatment. If you tell lies about him again, just see what I do to you! Your guardian will neither know nor care what happened to you.' Her tone is menacing and her eyes bulge in rage.

Harshita does not doubt that Anisha will kill her if she dares complain again.

The next Saturday, a weak Harshita, her body still recovering from the ordeal of the previous week, is sent to the fifth floor again. By the end of the month, Harshita is in too bad a shape to go to school and has to use the wall as support to shuffle around in her room She has lost bladder control and feels a terrible burning sensation whenever she pees. She also starts vomiting uncontrollably. Anisha and Srinath beat her up for soiling her bedsheets. But, worried, she sends Srinath to the pharmacy to bring her some medication. Harshita recovers slightly. But then, the weekly torture begins again. Satish is addicted to Harshita and is willing to pay large sums of money to get his fix.

Meanwhile, COVID-19 strikes. The orphanage is shut down. All the girls leave the orphanage. All the girls, *except* Harshita. When Harshita asks why she is not being allowed to leave, she is beaten up. She is not allowed to call her guardian.

Instead, Anisha lies that she had tried to call Samuel, but he is not interested in taking her back. Harshita is the wonderful cash cow that is allowing Anisha to build her dream home. How can she allow her to leave? When the orphanage inspector asks why Harshita has been kept back, Anisha says that she is keeping Harshita with her as she has nowhere else to go. She also mentions that she is thinking of adopting Harshita herself. She tells the inspector that as Harshita is in poor health, a cousin of hers, a doctor named Satish, comes occasionally to check up on her. The inspector allows Anisha to keep Harshita.

Two months later, Harshita is vomiting uncontrollably. No medications work on her. Finally, Anisha places a call to Samuel, her guardian. Samuel is shocked when he sees the sick Harshita. He takes her to a hospital despite his wife grumbling about him wasting money on Harshita when he wasn't earning enough to feed his own kids. A kind nurse at the hospital asks Harshita how she got so sick. Initially, Harshita is reluctant to say anything. But finally, after a lot of gentle nudging from the nurse, she reveals what has happened. The nurse calls the police. The police record her statement. She names Anisha and Srinath in her complaint.

She doesn't know the name of the man who molested her. But she had seen him give large donations to the orphanage. She, along with her friends Divya, Nandini and Urmila, sang songs when he visited the orphanage with his family to celebrate his daughter's birthday. She specifically mentions her friends Divya, Nandini and Urmila as witnesses to the suffering she experienced because of that man.

Two days later, Harshita dies of multiple-organ failure. Finally, she gets the freedom that Anisha, the manager of her orphanage, had denied her for so long. The police arrest Anisha and Srinath and start their investigations. Soon, they get the name of the man who raped and killed Harshita.

※

15 September 2020

The ACP, Crimes & SIT, Telangana Police, is personally conducting the interrogation. She holds a letter in her hands. She shows it to the girls.

'Is this Harshita's handwriting?' The ACP asks.

They nod.

'She wrote very good English for a fourteen-year-old girl,' she comments.

'Yes, ma'am,' Nandini says. 'She used to stand first in class. She told us that her mother wanted her to do well in studies. She herself wanted to be a writer.'

The ACP sighs. Then she pulls herself together. This is no

time to be emotional. The criminal—a vicious paedophile—is very influential and rich. But the ACP is determined that he be punished for the heinous crime he has committed. She will fast-track this case under the POCSO Act so that justice is meted out swiftly.

'Your friend Harshita is dead.' She tells the girls gently. 'Before she died, she gave your names as witnesses to what happened to her. Only you can help her get justice. Will you help the police? You have nothing to be afraid of. We will take care of you.'

The girls hesitate. Then Urmila, Harshita's best friend at the orphanage, says in a determined voice, 'I'll tell you.'

The other two take courage from her and nod.

'A man used to come to the orphanage,' Urmila says. 'He used to take Harshita to the fifth-floor bedroom.'

'Why to the fifth floor?'

'Ma'am, it was private. The residents of the orphanage are not allowed to go there,' Divya says.

'Okay. Do you know what happened there?'

'The first time it happened, the man left after some time. But Harshita did not come down for a long time. So, we went up to see what was wrong. We found her naked and unconscious.'

'What happened then?'

'She told us that this man was a doctor and that he had made her take a tablet. He said that she was weak and the tablet was a medicine that would make her strong. She said that she doesn't remember what happened after she took the tablet. She started vomiting after regaining consciousness and complained of intense pain in her private parts.'

'Hmm… Did she complain to the manager?' The ACP asks.

Urmila nods emphatically. 'She did. She told Anisha ma'am. But Anisha ma'am told her to keep her mouth shut. She beat her for vomiting and warned her that she would be beaten even more if she told anybody what this man had done to her.'

'So she didn't tell anybody other than you?'

The girls nod.

'And you kept quiet because you were afraid of Anisha ma'am?'

The girls nod again. 'We have nowhere else to go. We were afraid of antagonizing Anisha ma'am,' Urmila says.

Divya adds, 'But Harshita was becoming more and more sick whenever this man took her to the fifth-floor room. She didn't want to go. Every Saturday, she used to become so tense, so scared. She even tried to hide in the bathroom once. But ma'am forcibly took her to the fifth-floor room.'

Urmila nodded.

'Yes, ma'am. She used to tremble at the very thought of this man. And she became more and more sick. She started to vomit frequently; she would wet her bed and had a burning sensation whenever she passed urine. She also fainted once in the bathroom.'

'Yet Anisha ma'am didn't take her to the doctor for treatment?'

Urmila said with quiet anger. 'No, ma'am. Rather she

used to beat her up for wetting her bed and vomiting in the room.'

Nandini spoke up, 'She was a good student, ma'am. But she couldn't attend school regularly because she was so sick. Her grades began to fall. She was miserable, ma'am. But she didn't have anybody to turn to for help. We all knew that something bad was happening to her, yet none of us could do anything.'

'How long did this continue?' The ACP asks.

'It happened every Saturday from January till the time we were all sent home due to COVID. But Anisha ma'am didn't allow Harshita to go home during COVID, even though she wouldn't let anyone else stay.'

'Do you know who this man is?'

The girls shook their heads. 'We don't. But he had come with his family to the orphanage once on his daughter's birthday. We sang "Happy Birthday" for his daughter.'

The ACP took out a photo of Satish.

'Is this the man?'

They nodded in unison.

'This man used to regularly spend time with Anisha ma'am and her brother. They allowed him to take Harshita to the fifth-floor room. I saw this man handing cash to Anisha ma'am one day, when I went to give them tea in her office,' Divya says.

'So, Anisha ma'am ensured that Harshita stayed back even though the other residents in the orphanage went home when it was closed for COVID?'

'Yes, ma'am. Once we left, we had no way of knowing

what was going on with Harshita. We all were worried about her,' Divya says. The other girls nod in unison.

'And then, the police contacted my guardian and said that Harshita was dead.' Urmila starts to cry. Then she looks up in fright. 'Ma'am, will Anisha ma'am and her brother kill us too for telling you what really happened?'

༺༻

Satish is agitatedly pacing up and down in his impressively decorated, huge library-cum-home-office. He is unshaven and looks tired and drawn. When Rani tries to ask him why he is so restless, he snaps at her. Sensing that he is in one of his ugly rages, Rani quietly withdraws from the room.

Satish continues to pace up and down in the office, clutching his phone. He had received a message that Srinath somehow managed to send through a friend of his, warning him that the police were after him. Satish is a respectable man in society. Everybody knows where he lives, where he works. He has nowhere to run. Srinath's friend also informed him that Srinath had overheard the police saying that the case would be tried under the POCSO Act, and that the victim had left a statement incriminating him before dying. Cursing Harshita for not dying before her statement could be recorded, he calls up the most expensive lawyer in town.

༺༻

Rani cannot believe her eyes when the police come to arrest her husband.

'You are wrong!' She keeps saying. 'My Satish can't be like that.'

Satish himself doesn't say anything. He gives Rani the number of the lawyer he has hired and asks her to call him and update him about his arrest. Rani calls the lawyer obediently. Then she goes to Lakshmi's school to pick her up.

Lakshmi asks, 'Where are we going, ma?'

Rani looks at her and says, 'We are going to Vizag, to visit your grandparents.'

Lakshmi is initially delighted; she loves being pampered by her maternal grandparents. But she is a sharp girl and notices that her mother has been crying. 'Why didn't you tell me before?' She demands. 'And what about our luggage? Have you fought with papa?'

'Yes,' Rani lies.

'But what about papa? Who will take care of him?' Lakshmi's face crumples in distress for her beloved father.

'He will join us soon,' Rani assures her.

They reach Vizag after twelve hours of non-stop driving. Lakshmi is tired and sleepy when they reach Rani's parents' house.

Rani's mother is surprised but happy to see her. Her joy turns to concern when she realizes that they have not brought any luggage. 'What happened? Everything okay?' She asks, studying Rani's drawn and tired face.

'Yes, we are fine,' Rani responds mechanically. 'Will you

take care of Lakshmi? I have some work. I'll come back in some time.'

Her mother is astonished, but Rani runs out before she can ask anything.

Rani walks for miles, leaving the city far behind. Her phone vibrates. It is the latest iPhone that her husband gifted her with so much love. Or so she had thought. The phone is on silent, but the buzzing persists. It must be her mother. She pulls it from her bag and, without looking at the screen, drops it into the ditch beside her, where it splashes into a pool of stagnant water. She pulls off her diamond jewellery and drops it into the ditch too, along with her Apple watch. The last connection to her husband has been cut, and almost immediately she feels free. Her feet start to ache and she knows that if she were to stop and lie down on the road, she would never get up. It must be late in the night, she thinks. It is dark and silent in the narrow, empty road, as if she were the only remaining person in this world. All she can hear is her own breathing and she begins to feel calmer. She doesn't let herself think about what has happened or where she is going. She just walks.

Suddenly, she hears a car behind her. It overtakes her, then slows down about five metres ahead. There is a faint hiss from the brakes and the smell of exhaust. Blood pounds in her ears and she turns and clumsily runs back the way she came, her blistered feet rubbing against her trainers, sweat trickling down her back and between her breasts.

Two men drunkenly climb out of the car and holler after her, '*Medam*, lift?'

Rani doesn't respond; she just runs faster. What will happen to her daughter if she dies? Will Lakshmi end up in an orphanage and be pushed straight into the arms of a monster like Satish? Rani has to live, if only for her daughter. After running for what seems like hours, she looks back timidly. Nobody is following her. She is safe.

She knocks softly on her parents' door. Her mother flings it open. She opens her mouth to demand answers, but one look at Rani's face, and she stops talking and embraces her daughter.

A tsunami of emotion engulfs Rani with such force that she can barely breathe. The grief that she feels is violent and physical. Her heart continues to beat even though it has been wrenched apart. Big, fat tears stream down from her eyes, drenching her mother's cotton saree.

∞

India Daily News

Thursday, 15 February 2021. Last updated: 17:20 IST.

Tragic Case of Sexual Assault Ends with Justice Served under POCSO Act

By Rituparna Chakraborty

A distressing incident of sexual assault has come to light, highlighting the importance of the Protection of Children from Sexual Offences (POCSO) Act in delivering justice to young victims.

Harshita, a fourteen-year-old resident of the Sreedevi Orphanage in Vikrampuri, was brutally raped by Mr Satish, who used to drug her using a date-rape substance. Satish subjected Harshita to repeated sexual abuse over a period of six months. The proprietor of the orphanage Ms M. Anisha and her brother Srinath were bribed by Mr Satish to ensure their silence.

The severity of the assaults took a terrible toll on Harshita's health, leaving her in an extremely debilitated state. Concerned about the consequences, the perpetrators sent her to her legal guardian's place under the pretext of seeking medical assistance. Harshita initially didn't want to tell what had actually happened to her. However, after some cajoling from the nurse of the hospital and some reassurances that nobody would blame her, she revealed the harrowing and shocking details of the repeated rapes committed by Mr Satish.

Her physical condition also showed her claims to be true: she had difficulty walking, incontinence, and intense pain in the genital area. After listening to Harshita's confession, the nurse went straight to the police and filed a report.

Sadly, despite medical intervention, Harshita's condition deteriorated rapidly, and she passed away in the hospital. However, right before she died, she gave a statement of the atrocities that were committed against her and this was important evidence in the subsequent court case.

A case was registered by the ACP, Crimes & SIT, Hyderabad Police, under the POCSO Act, which focuses on protecting children from sexual offences. Within six

In the Name of the Children

months, the perpetrator, Mr Satish, was found guilty and sentenced to rigorous imprisonment for life. When we went to Mr Satish's home to meet his wife, we found the house locked up. Nobody had stayed there for the past six months. Satish's parents denied that he had committed any crime. 'He is a good human being who is incapable of committing such dastardly crimes. He has a small girl of his own whom he loves. How can anybody even think that he would rape a girl of his child's age? It's ridiculous! We will go to the Supreme Court,' his mother told *India Daily News*. Satish's office declined to provide any comments regarding his actions, citing the sensitivity and gravity of the situation. They also mentioned that he had resigned and was no longer associated with the company.

I Will Never Let You Go

25 April 2019

Amruta's heart beat erratically as she wondered about her daughter Renuka. She held the teddy bear that Renuka, though now fourteen years old, still slept with and cuddled every night. At times, Amruta hugged the toy and smelled it, for it had Renuka's smell. She had been a very happy woman when Renuka was born, especially after having two boys before her. The sunset cast red and yellow lights through the window but all that this did was make Amruta feel anxious and uneasy in her heart. Renuka was missing since the afternoon. She usually came home from school by 12.30 p.m., regular as clockwork. But today, it was 4.00 p.m. and there was still no trace of Renuka.

Amruta's hands clutched a crumpled handkerchief with which she kept wiping her tears. With every passing minute, the weight of uncertainty pressed heavier on her shoulders. Her sons, Sravan and Pavan, alongside their friends and acquaintances in the village, had set out in search of Renuka. They had formed groups of two or three people and were scouring all the desolate places in the village, like the abandoned Shiva temple. They had already searched every inch of the fields and bushes that lined the two sides of the unpaved road that lead from Deverakonda to Gazipur. Deverakonda was the last place till where autos were willing to come. After that, one had to walk about two kilometres to reach their house in Gazipur.

'Why did I let her go alone so far to school?' Amruta scolded herself, slapping her forehead. 'I should have kept her close. God alone knows where she is! Durga amma, please keep my daughter safe, I beg of you.'

She recalled how irritated Renuka had been when Amruta packed some *pulihora* in her steel tiffin box.

Renuka had complained, 'Why do you give me the same tamarind rice for tiffin every single day, amma?'

Amruta had responded with irritation, 'Can't you see that I have too much work? When will you be a little more sensitive to your mother's hardships? This is the best I can do so early in the morning. Now I'll have to prepare breakfast and lunch for your brothers and father, and then go to help in the fields. I'm not feeling too well myself.'

Renuka was immediately contrite. 'I'm sorry, amma,' she said, embracing her mother.

Renuka could speak good English and her mother was very proud of her. Amruta had always had a fascination for people who spoke good English. She herself had never got a chance to go to school, but she wanted her children to be well educated. Renuka was good in studies and Amruta was proud of the sincerity her daughter showed.

Candle in the Wind

The anxious wait for Renuka's return, the restless pacing up and down the veranda, the frequent glances thrown at the road leading to the village—Amruta's ears strained for any sound that could bring her hope—a familiar voice, the footsteps that should have brought her daughter home.

When Sravan, Pavan and their friends who had gone in search of Renuka returned, there was no sign of success on their tired, worried faces. The knot in Amruta's stomach tightened. She clung to the teddy bear, as if by doing so she could get Renuka back into her arms. Soon it was night and most of the folks around her fell asleep. But Amruta could not sleep. She felt like the walls of despair were closing in on her. As the moon rose high in the sky, Amruta stood in the doorway as if hoping to see her daughter return magically. 'Govinda! I'll do anything; I'll do everything for Renuka's safe return,' she uttered, weeping inconsolably. 'I beg of you, don't take her away from me.'

∽

Meanwhile, the villagers got together to speculate on what might have happened to Renuka; whether she had run away with a boyfriend. Village gossip had it that Renuka was very close to a young man called Sunil, who was studying BCom in a college in Nalgonda where Renuka's school was also located. Nalgonda was a small town about a quarter-of-an-hour away from the village. The gossip soon reached the ears of Prakash, Renuka's father, who promptly went to confront Sunil's parents. When he knocked on their door, to his great surprise, Sunil himself opened the door. He had a black eye, and there were scratches on his face and arms.

'What happened?' Prakash asked him, pointing to the wounds.

'Oh, I got into a fight with some bullies in my college who were trying to rag me. It's nothing.'

But Prakash immediately grew suspicious. Had Sunil attacked Renuka and had she fought back, causing these wounds? Still, he couldn't voice his suspicions so openly.

'Have you seen Renuka? She hasn't come home since yesterday,' Prakash asked instead.

Sunil appeared genuinely surprised. 'I had no idea she was missing. I spent the entire day at home resting after yesterday's altercation. So I wasn't aware of this situation. Renuka is like a younger sister to me, uncle. Our interactions were limited to brief greetings when we crossed paths while she was en route to school and I, to college. Just simple exchanges of "hi" and "hello", nothing more. Occasionally, since I travelled to college by motorcycle, I would offer her a ride to Deverakonda, from where she would catch an auto to her school.'

After talking to Sunil, Prakash proceeded to the Nalgonda Police Station. He filed a complaint regarding Renuka's disappearance and also voiced his suspicions about Sunil. 'He has recently been involved in a fight. I noticed scratches on his face, and he has a black eye. He says he got into a fight with his friends but I think these wounds were inflicted when Renuka attacked him in self-defence. Please, *please* sir…please arrest him. Maybe we can save Renuka.'

The police seemed to think that Renuka might have run away with a boyfriend. 'This is common teenage behaviour these days, nothing to worry about. You will hear from her in a day or two,' they assured Prakash.

Prakash was deeply offended by the police's assumption. He said forcefully, 'Renuka was a good girl, and we were absolutely devoted to her. There's absolutely no reason for her to run away from her home. She was a sincere student and had no time for love-shove!'

'But you yourself told us about Sunil!' The officer-in-charge shot back.

'I never said that he was her boyfriend. I believe he might have been stalking her. Maybe he tried to kidnap her and she fought back. Maybe that's how he got the scratches.'

After much persuasion, the police promised to start the enquiry if Renuka was not found within the next twenty-four hours. They also promised to interrogate Sunil and find out how he had sustained the injuries on his body.

Prakash was frustrated by what he thought was typical police apathy and inaction. He decided to retrace Renuka's movements on the day of her disappearance. But Renuka's school was already closed for the day. 'I should have enquired at her school instead of fruitlessly searching around in the village and wasting time,' he thought ruefully to himself.

When he reached home, he told Amruta that he had a nagging suspicion that Sunil was responsible for Renuka's disappearance. 'Are you aware if Renuka was having some kind of affair with Sunil?' He asked Amruta.

'Of course not!' Amruta snapped. 'How can you even

think like that. Renuka was a sweet and innocent child. She was dedicated to her studies and had no time for the advances of small-time village folks like Sunil.'

'But the village gossips...' Prakash objected.

'What do they know about my daughter?' Renuka said indignantly. 'Renuka wanted to become a doctor and had no time for these loafers from the village. She herself used to tell me that she was destined for bigger things in life, far beyond the narrow confines of the village.'

∞

26 April 2019

The following day, Prakash visited the school with the intention of retracing Renuka's journey back from school. Despite the official study holidays due to the upcoming board exams, the school had arranged extra classes for the more promising students who could benefit from the extra tuitions. The teachers confirmed that Renuka had attended these classes the previous day.

Renuka's best friends, Sravani and Madhavi, told Prakash that they all took the same auto back home after attending classes. Prakash grilled them about Renuka's relationship with Sunil. 'Did she meet him secretly? Please tell me if you know anything. It will help the police find her,' he pleaded with them. But both of them denied any relationship between Renuka and Sunil. Prakash even made them swear on Goddess Saraswati, but they stuck to what they said. With their help, Prakash located the auto driver who had taken them back from school yesterday. The auto was part of a group of shared autos that operated between Nalgonda and Lalaguda, the village adjacent to Deverakonda.

The driver informed Prakash that he had first dropped Sravani, who lived closest to the school at the Anjaneya Swami Temple bus stop. Around ten minutes later, Madhavi had got off at the Pedda Parvatapura bus stop. Renuka's stop in Deverakonda was the final one, another ten minutes past Madhavi's stop. After Renuka's drop-off, the auto driver had one final passenger whom he took to Lalaguda. There, he had waited in the shared auto queue till he found passengers heading back towards Nalgonda. Sravani and Madhavi confirmed the driver's account.

Prakash requested the auto driver to take him to the exact spot where he had dropped off Renuka. After some haggling, Prakash agreed to pay the driver two hundred rupees for this favour. While they were on their way, Prakash's mind started to wander. He began to doubt whether the driver was being truthful about what happened after he dropped off Madhavi. Questions plagued him—what if the other passenger had actually disembarked before Renuka and she was alone in the auto? Could the driver have done something to Renuka? Despite the driver's apparent sympathy, Prakash couldn't help but consider the possibility that it was all an act. To be cautious, he saved the driver's name and phone number and called him once to verify its accuracy, intending to share this information with the police.

I Will Never Let You Go

The auto driver dropped Prakash off at the same spot where he had dropped Renuka the day before—a shady area beneath a tamarind tree in Deverakonda. He offered to stay back and help Prakash search for Renuka. But Prakash refused his help. The driver shrugged and turned his auto back towards Nalgonda. As Prakash stood beneath the tamarind tree, he felt devastated. Where was Renuka? What had befallen his innocent child? As he glanced around, unsure of his next steps, he sensed someone watching him. His attention was drawn to a house near the tamarind tree, where an elderly lady sat on the doorstep, observing him curiously. Approaching her, he showed a photo of Renuka.

'Amma, did you see this child yesterday afternoon?' He asked.

He was elated when the old lady confirmed that she had seen Renuka. 'Yes, I even asked her what her name was and what she was doing alone in the middle of the afternoon. The child told me her name was Renuka and that she was going back to her home in Gazipur after attending school in Nalgonda.'

'Was she alone?' Prakash asked.

'Yes, yes... She was alone,' the old lady confirmed.

'Did it look like she was waiting for someone?' Prakash asked again.

'I asked her the same question. She said that she was waiting to see if she could find someone going towards her village on a cycle or bike. She wanted to grab a lift. It was really too hot to walk, I must say.'

Prakash nodded. Many adults in their small village in

Gazipur had their own bikes, mopeds or scooties, and school children often asked for lifts from them to avoid walking the additional two kilometres to their village carrying their heavy school bags.

'Did she get a lift? Or did she walk back from here?' Prakash asked.

The old lady scratched her head. 'That I don't know,' she said ruefully. 'It was very hot and I was feeling thirsty. So I went inside to drink a glass of water. When I came out again, she was gone.'

This piece of information told Prakash that Renuka had reached the outskirts of their village around 12.30 p.m. After that, however, there was no trace of her.

It was 3.30 p.m. on the day after Renuka's disappearance. As the police were not taking any action even after Prakash had filed a complaint, the villagers took matters in their own hands.

The search for Renuka intensified as her friends and other villagers continued to scour the area, fear and desperation palpable in their hearts. Senthil, Sravan's friend, was a member of the search party, driven by a sense of duty to find the young girl. As he passed a dried-up well, known locally as the Marri Bavi, something made him look into the well. What if Renuka had accidentally fallen in? He leaned inside and looked into the depth of the dry well. What he saw froze his heart. It was quite dark. But he saw what looked like a school bag lying at the bottom of the well. He switched on the torch of his mobile and focused it on the object. Yes…it was a school bag, which had obviously been thrown in recently because it looked clean.

Looking around the well, his eyes fell on three beer bottles and some cigarette butts lying under the shade of a nearby neem tree. A shiver ran down his spine as he noticed the telltale signs of revelry. Something was terribly wrong. Senthil rushed to inform Prakash.

Even as he was relaying what he had found, Prakash got a call from some villagers in the Tatte Bavi area; a foul smell was emanating from another forty-six-feet deep, dried-up well that was about half a kilometre from the Marri Bavi. This well was also located in a deserted area that the locals hardly visited. Senthil, Prakash and Renuka's brothers—Pavan and Sravan—rushed to the Tatte Bavi.

As they approached, the murmurs of the villagers gathered around the well reached their ears. The air was heavy with trepidation, with the fading light only adding to the sense of dread. Sravan gagged at the horrible stench emanating from the well. Senthil peered into the dark void but saw nothing. He volunteered to climb down to the bottom of the well. There were iron rungs along its wall which could be used as a ladder.

Senthil steeled his resolve and began to climb down, carefully feeling for the rungs with his feet. The well, similar to the Marri Bavi well, was about four storeys deep. The stench got worse with every step he took; he wished he had tied a handkerchief over his mouth and nose. The sun was setting and darkness would soon settle over the village. Despite the moderate light outside, it was dark and eerie inside the well. The voices of the villagers floated faintly

Candle in the Wind

down to Senthil. Reaching the bottom, he switched on the mobile's torch. The stench was overbearing, and he felt terrified despite the crowd watching from above. Sweat poured down his body in rivulets even though it was cool at this depth. He covered his nose with his left hand and scanned the well with his mobile torch. He noticed a mound of gravel and poked it with his foot. Some gravel fell away and he could see that something was buried beneath. His heart pounded in his chest and his breath came in shallow gasps. Holding the mobile torch in his shaking hand, he scooped away the gravel, revealing Renuka's lifeless face. Her eyes were wide open and bulging, and her rigid tongue jutted out. It seemed as though, in her final moments, she had wanted to scream defiance at the cruel and violent world. Senthil dropped the mobile in shock and the light switched off. Senthil puked and then began to scream, his terrified voice echoing in the closed well. The villagers shouted back, 'What? What happened?'

'Renu...' Senthil couldn't complete the words as he started to heave.

∞

The village was in shock. Even the moon hid behind a veil of clouds, as if unable to bear witness to the evil that had befallen the innocent girl. The horror of that night would forever scar the hearts and minds of all who saw Renuka, their once-bright hopes now dimmed by darkness.

The search for Renuka had ended in tragedy, and the

quest for justice would now begin, though no amount of retribution could ever heal the wounds left behind.

Additional District Superintendent of Police N. Bhujanga Rao arrived at the scene within the hour, accompanied by his team of constables and sub-inspectors. A farmer named Raghuveer provided a generator and a focus light. The police removed the dirt and gravel and unearthed the naked body of Renuka. Buried with her were her clothes—her blue salwar-kameez school uniform and a brown panty. There were blood stains on her panty.

Then they found a second grave, which was at a greater depth. The body in this grave must have been buried a few months back as all that remained was a skeleton which was clothed in a saree and a blouse—the kind a young girl would wear. They also recovered the bag of the young girl with her college ID card—Swapna, a seventeen-year-old BCom student of Nalgonda College.

ADSP Bhujanga Rao suspected that these crimes might have been committed by a serial killer. This violent individual was killing and burying young girls in dried-up wells in the region. Renuka's body and Swapna's skeleton were sent to the nearby government hospital for post-mortem.

When Senthil told the police about Renuka's school bag in the Marri Bavi well, they recovered that too, alongside the beer bottles and the cigarette butts. Most probably, the killer had smoked and drunk beer sitting under the neem tree after committing his heinous crimes. They would collect fingerprints from the school bag and the beer bottles, and DNA from the cigarette butts.

If these crimes were indeed the work of a serial killer, it was imperative that they found him before he could harm more young girls.

Somebody in the village had secretly recorded the bodies being dug out of the well and carried into an ambulance. The person also recorded the police taking away Renuka's school bag from the bottom of the Marri Bavi well, and collecting the beer bottles and cigarette butts from the ground beneath the neem tree. A police constable let slip that Rao thought this could be the work of a serial killer. The video was then uploaded on Facebook and shared via WhatsApp. Soon it went viral; the news that a possible serial killer was on the loose in Gazipur village spread like wildfire.

∞

When the news of Renuka's brutal death reached Amruta's ears, she fainted. She woke up to see her best friend, Shalini, sprinkling water on her face. For a moment, she didn't know what had happened, and then she remembered. Renuka! Renuka! Her only girl child—whom she had loved and cherished so much, whom she had treated like a little doll—was dead! Brutally raped and killed, and buried inside a well. The very thought of what her child had endured ripped Amruta's heart apart, plunging her into the depths of indescribable grief.

She was aware that Shalini was saying something, but her words didn't penetrate her mind. She wished Shalini would leave her alone so that she could grieve in peace. 'Go away!' She shouted. Shalini sighed, but wouldn't budge from the chair beside the bed. Amruta turned on her side and shut her out, even though she realized that Shalini meant well. All she could think of was why such a terrible fate had befallen her innocent child. She cried out to God, pleading for an answer. 'Oh Govinda!' She wailed. 'How could you be so cruel? Why didn't you take my life instead of Renuka's?'

As her mind struggled to understand the cruelty and heartlessness of the system that had taken her daughter's life, Amruta's grief turned into an insatiable thirst for justice. Someone had caused irretrievable damage to her Renuka and that person would have to pay.

∞

The Investigation Begins: 27 April 2019

As this was an extremely grave case of a serial killer targeting young girls indiscriminately, it was transferred to the Additional Commissioner of Police, Crimes & SIT.

By then, newspapers had sniffed out the story; it was making headlines. Soon, the paparazzi and YouTubers descended on the village with their crew and cameras, trying to fish out more news from the locals. A local constable with a loose mouth informed some reporters that the case had been transferred to Crimes & SIT. Those reporters tried to contact the ACP, but she managed to avoid them.

She set up a meeting with the Commissioner of Police and updated him personally about the case. The CP, who had high regard for his capable deputy, listened attentively.

'If this is really a case of serial killing, it is not going to be easy,' she warned the CP. 'By and large, the victims are killed by people whom they know and who have some personal motive to kill them. Most of the time, the crime is committed in the heat of the moment and little, if anything, is done to avoid leaving evidence or witnesses behind. Serial killers, on the other hand, have no connection whatsoever to their victims, so even if they leave forensic evidence, they cannot be traced easily. It will be a difficult case to solve.'

'Try your best, ma'am,' the CP said with a smile. 'Given your track record, I'm sure you will be successful in solving this case.'

'Yes sir.' The ACP saluted him smartly and left his office.

She immediately set out for Gazipur. On the way, she studied the file that had been sent to her by the Nalgonda police and memorized the names of the victim and her family members.

The people of the village were very agitated. They gathered around her police car as soon as she arrived at the Tatte Bavi well.

The local constables were shooing the villagers away sternly, but the ACP stopped them. She smiled at the angry villagers and assured them that the police were fully focused on finding the perpetrator.

'We are trying to solve the case as soon as possible. This

type of horrible crime against women will not go unsolved. The killer will be caught and punished, I promise. Now tell me, who saw the body first?'

Senthil stepped forward shyly. He was impressed by the lady police officer and was eager to cooperate. He told her how he had first noticed Renuka's school bag and afterwards climbed down the Tatte Bavi well and discovered the body.

'Did you know Renuka?' The ACP asked in Telugu.

'Yes, ma'am,' he said, with a slight smile at her accent. 'She was my friend Sravan's younger sister. She was very good in studies.'

'You are a very observant boy. You correctly took note of the beer bottles and the cigarette butts. But you didn't touch them, thus preserving the fingerprints. Very good.'

Senthil blushed with pride. He watched the *CID* TV series whenever he got the opportunity and was aware of criminal investigation procedures. After meeting this inspiring police officer, he decided on the spot that he would join the police force after his graduation.

The ACP was speaking to the other villagers. 'Okay, let me know if any of you saw or remember anything else in relation to Renuka's disappearance.'

Turning to Senthil, she asked, 'Can you take us to the Marri Bavi where you found Renuka's school bag?'

Senthil proudly sat in the front seat of the ACP's Innova and directed the driver to the Marri Bavi. There, he pointed excitedly at the neem tree where he had noticed the beer bottles.

After thanking him and praising him again for his keen

observation, the ACP turned to the next task that faced her. Meeting the grieving parents of young murder victims was by far the most gut-wrenching part of her job. It tore at her soul, but she could not shirk this weighty responsibility. She knew there were no words in the world that could truly console the inconsolable, but she had to be there—to listen and provide whatever strength and solace she could. In their insurmountable grief, the parents would look to her for justice, and it was her duty to assure them of it.

She squared her shoulders. 'Hussein,' she said to her driver, 'let's go to the child's home. I have to meet the parents.' The living room of Renuka's house was filled with grief-stricken relatives and friends. Amruta sat on the sofa, her hands trembling with shock and sorrow. The ACP approached her respectfully.

She said softly, 'Mrs Amruta, I am the ACP, Crimes & SIT, and the lead investigator of this case. I cannot even begin to imagine the pain and loss you are going through right now. Please accept my heartfelt condolences.'

Amruta's eyes were red and swollen from crying. With a sob, she said, 'Thank you, Madam. It's just...it's unbearable. Renuka was my world, and she was taken from us so brutally.'

The ACP sighed. 'I can't fathom the depth of your grief, but I want you to know that I am here for you and your family. We will do everything in our power to find whoever is responsible for this heinous act and bring them to justice. Renuka will not be forgotten and her killer will be held accountable.'

Amruta looked up at the ACP. Her powerful presence and upright demeanour commanded respect. Amruta realized even in the middle of her sorrow that with this lady at the helm, justice would be served. With folded hands, she said, 'Please, ma'am, you have to find this horrible person. Renuka was just a child...innocent and full of life. Oh, what pain she must have gone through.' Amruta shuddered and started to sob uncontrollably. Her husband, who had been sitting stone-faced beside her, said, 'Don't cry, Amruta. Madam here will surely catch her killer.'

The ACP turned towards Prakash and said resolutely, 'You have my word, Prakash garu. My team and I will leave no stone unturned in our investigation. We will follow every lead, examine every piece of evidence, and work tirelessly to apprehend the perpetrator. I promise you, justice will be served.'

Amruta looked at the ACP, a glimmer of hope amidst the darkness of her grief. Composing herself, she said in a stronger voice, 'Thank you, ACP madam. It means a lot to us that you're taking this case seriously.'

The ACP put a hand on Amruta's shoulder. 'I can't ease your pain right now, but I hope that knowing we're doing everything we can will give you some comfort. Please remember, you're not alone in this. If you need anything at all, even just someone to talk to, I'm here for you and your husband.' The ACP looked around the room. 'I'll leave you with your family for now, but I'll be in touch regularly to update you on our progress. And please, if you remember anything, no matter how insignificant it may seem, don't hesitate to let us know.' Prakash and Amruta nodded earnestly. After the utter bleakness of the previous few days, they felt their first sense of relief, knowing that there was a dedicated officer who would be working tirelessly to catch their daughter's killer.

∞

After meeting the parents, the ACP went to the Nalgonda Police Station and called a meeting with ADSP Bhujanga Rao and the members of his team who had been involved in exhuming Renuka's body and Swapna's skeleton.

'Has Renuka's body been identified by her parents?' The ACP asked.

'Yes, ma'am,' Rao said. 'We have taken official statements from her father in front of witnesses.'

'Good. And what about Swapna, the college student?'

'We have traced her parents too. We have taken blood samples from them to match with the DNA of the skeleton. We have sent the same to forensics for confirmation. But Swapna's father has identified her clothes and bag that were buried with her.'

'Why was she never reported missing?'

'She was the youngest of four daughters, left vulnerable after their mother's recent demise. The others were already married, leaving her alone with her father, Srinivas. But within just six months of their mother's passing, Srinivas remarried, and from that point on, Swapna's life took a dark turn. She clashed relentlessly with her stepmother, and at one point, she fled to her aunt's home, staying away for ten days. So, when she went missing again, Srinivas assumed it was another act of rebellion, just like before.'

'But the girl must have been buried in that well for at least six months!' The ACP exclaimed.

Constable Tarun, who had helped exhume Swapna's skeleton, smiled sadly. 'That's the unfortunate reality for women in these villages, ma'am. When the daughter disappeared, the father washed his hands of her. He was relieved that he would not have to spend any more money on her education or subsequent marriage.'

A deep sigh escaped the ACP's lips, her seasoned heart shaken by the depth of callousness to which some people fall. No matter how long she had already served in the police force, the lack of humanity in people continued to shock and deeply disgust her. She was grateful to God that her parents had always treated her and her brothers equally, ensuring that they were given equal opportunities in life.

She looked at Rao and asked, 'What makes you so certain that this is the work of a serial killer? Do we know of any other girls who have gone missing in that area?'

'Only these two girls as of now, ma'am.'

Constable Tarun commented, 'Swapna's skeleton was fully clothed and she was buried in a much deeper grave. But in Renuka's case, the killer carelessly piled her clothes on top of her body and simply dumped mud and gravel on the body. There are slight differences between the two murders.'

Constable Balakrishna, not to be outdone by Tarun, said, 'And the bags. He had buried Swapna's bag along with her in the grave. But in Renuka's case, he simply threw the bag in another well.'

The ACP shrugged. 'It simply shows that the killer is becoming more confident and callous. I feel that he was more cautious when he killed Swapna. Maybe she was one of his earlier victims. He grew complacent after he got away with Swapna's murder. I wouldn't be surprised if he committed a few more murders after killing Swapna and got away with those.'

Rao nodded. 'You're probably right. A dangerous person is roaming around the village. We must warn all the families as soon as possible.'

He looked at his team and pointed to Tarun and Balakrishna. 'Both of you. After this meeting, go to Gazipur and inform the villagers of the potential danger.'

Tarun and Balakrishna nodded.

Balakrishna said, 'But ma'am, you didn't answer my question.'

The ACP looked at him. 'What was the question?'

'Why did the killer bury Renuka in Tatte Bavi and throw her bag in Marri Bavi?'

The ACP didn't respond immediately. She thought for a while, pinching her chin with her index finger and thumb. Then she nodded to herself and said, 'I don't know exactly why he did what he did. I can only make an educated guess. As I told you, he has become more callous and careless. He took the body down to the well, carelessly piled gravel

I Will Never Let You Go

on the body and came out of the well. Then he noticed that he had forgotten to bury her bag along with her. He didn't feel like climbing back into the well again. So he probably thought he would simply throw the bag into the well. But then caution prevailed. If he threw the bag into the well and if somebody looked into the well, they would see the bag and perhaps climb down to recover it. Then they would definitely notice the body. So he decided that he would hide the bag somewhere else. He went to the neem tree with his beer and, while smoking and drinking, he wondered where he could hide the bag. He could see the Marri Bavi from where he was sitting. He decided to simply throw the bag in there.'

'Didn't he worry that somebody would spot the bag? And somebody did. Senthil, that village boy.'

'Yes, probably he was drunk and grew careless. As I told you before, serial killers grow more and more confident and careless as they get away with more and more murders. That's what must have happened in this case. But we will get to know for sure only when we catch him.'

Rao noted the confidence in the ACP's voice and the choice of her words. She said, '*when* we catch him' and not '*if* we catch him'. He hoped that he would be able to live up to her expectations.

'Two minor girls buried in a deep well. Bag hidden in another well. The killer seems to have a fascination for wells.'

'Very good analysis, Rao,' the ACP said in an encouraging voice. 'Contact other nearby police stations. See if there are more minor girls who have been reported missing. Go to the wells again and check if there are more buried bodies. If we assume that there's a serial killer on the loose, then perhaps the killer is from that area only.'

'Why do you say that, ma'am?' Bhujanga Rao asked in surprise.

The ACP walked over to the whiteboard in the conference room where the meeting was taking place and wrote:

Knowledge of escape routes
Awareness of hiding places
Avoiding suspicion
Selection of victims

When she turned from the board, she was greeted by confused faces.

'Serial killers often tend to operate in familiar areas where they feel comfortable,' she explained. 'The reason for this is that familiarity with the location gives them several advantages and allows them to continue their crimes undetected.' She turned to tap the board with a pointer. 'Let's look at the first point. The serial killer is always worried about being caught. Familiarity with the area allows him to know the best escape routes to avoid capture after committing a crime.'

'Ma'am, you are assuming that the serial killer is a man. It could be a woman also, no?' Constable Balakrishna said.

The ACP sighed. 'What's your name?'

'Balakrishna, ma'am,' the constable muttered.

'Use your brains, Balakrishna. The girls have obviously been raped before they were killed. The killer has to be a man and a disgusting paedophile. There can be no doubt about that.'

The ACP looked at Rao. 'That reminds me. Have the autopsy results come in for Renuka? She was discovered just a day after her death, so the doctor should be able to tell us if she was raped. Also, forensics should be able to tell us if there are traces of the killer's DNA.'

Rao nodded. 'Yes, ma'am. We had sent the body for the post-mortem. I am expecting the results soon.'

'And what about forensics?'

'Yes, ma'am. We bagged both Swapna's and Renuka's clothes and have sent them for forensic analysis. We have also sent their bags for forensic analysis, along with the beer bottles and the cigarette butts. They will be tested for DNA and finger printing.'

'Good, good.' The ACP rubbed her hands together in satisfaction. Rao was doing a good job.

Constable Balakrishna said, 'Ma'am, you were explaining why serial killers like to operate in familiar territory.'

The ACP looked back at the board. 'Ah, yes. Let's take the second point, hiding places. Serial killers are more likely to be familiar with the local terrain, including potential hiding places for the bodies. In this case, both the girls were raped near Tatte Bavi. That well is hidden from public view due to the abundant growth of trees and shrubs around it. Locals don't go there either as the well is dry and the land around fallow. The killer must have known this. That's why he took both the girls there. Then he buried the bodies in the well. So he must be a strong, presentable young man.'

'Why ma'am?' Balakrishna asked.

'I'll say strong and agile, because he physically threw the girls' bodies into the well after raping and killing them. He then climbed down to the bottom of the deep well. This makes him agile. In the case of Swapna, he dug a deeper grave than Renuka. This would again make him strong.'

'How do you guess that he is a presentable person?' Tarun asked.

'Because he approached the girls and somehow they didn't get scared. But on what pretext did he approach the girls? Most probably he offered them lifts from Deverakonda to the village.'

'Ma'am, he might have forcibly kidnapped them, no?' Constable Balakrishna said.

'I don't think so. You see, Renuka was last seen at 12.30 in the afternoon in Deverakonda. It was broad daylight, and lots of buses and autos were passing by. It is difficult to kidnap someone under such conditions. If he had tried to kidnap Renuka, she would have created a ruckus. If nothing else, the old lady, who had noticed her, would have heard her.'

'Right, ma'am,' Balakrishna nodded.

The ACP nodded. 'That makes me think that he is a young man of decent appearance. And as I said before, he is a local and most probably these girls either knew him or were acquainted with him. He most likely has his own vehicle, either a bicycle or a bike on which he offered lifts.'

'When Renuka's father Prakash filed the missing person's complaint with us, he had mentioned a boy named Sunil

I Will Never Let You Go

who stays in the village. It seems that he had scratch marks all over his face and a black eye. Prakash mentioned that there was gossip among the villagers that Sunil was Renuka's boyfriend as they had seen Renuka on his bike sometimes. But when Prakash asked Sunil about this, he denied any such relationship. He said that Renuka was like his little sister and that he sometimes used to give her a lift till Deverakonda, from where she took an auto to her school.'

The ACP was excited at this news. 'This guy Sunil seems to match the profile that we are developing. I think that we should grill him thoroughly.'

She turned back to the board and pointed to the third bullet point. 'Now, coming to the next point of avoiding suspicion. Being a part of the local community or having connections in the area can help the killer blend in, making him less conspicuous and less likely to raise suspicion among locals or law-enforcement authorities. So, I suggest that you go back to the village and search for a young man of fairly decent appearance.'

Rao said, 'I think I understand what you mean by your next bullet-point, "Selection of victim". If he is a local, he can select victims whose disappearance wouldn't lead to police complaints. Like Swapna. He must have known that Swapna's stepmother and father would be relieved if she disappeared off the face of the earth, and would not raise a hue and cry. So he selected Swapna as his victim.'

Balakrishna raised his hand. 'Yes, Bala?' Rao raised his eyebrows a bit impatiently.

'Sir, if he is a local, then why did he go after Renuka?

Surely he would have known that she would be missed immediately.'

'Excellent point, Balakrishna. That makes me think that he has killed a few more girls.'

'He has killed more?' Balakrishna exclaimed.

'Yes, he has. The more people serial killers kill, the more intense their desire to kill grows. For them, killing is addictive. Like a drug addict craves drugs, they crave victims. So, even though he knew that Renuka would be immediately missed, he couldn't stop himself. And the other thing is, he has gotten away with so many murders. As I stressed before, he became careless. He buried the body in Tatte Bhavi and piled gravel on top of it, assuming that nobody would ever find it. Then he threw Renuka's school bag into another well nearby where it was easily visible. He left his DNA and fingerprints on cigarette butts and beer bottles that he carelessly discarded nearby. I'm sure that the DNA and fingerprints on the bottles will match those on the school bag.'

Rao agreed with a nod. 'Indeed, his negligence was evident. By merely dumping gravel over Renuka's body during such warm weather, instead of properly burying her in a deep grave, an unpleasant odour arose, effectively revealing the corpse's whereabouts.'

The ACP smiled. 'Very good, Rao garu. We are narrowing down our field of search. We will need to look for a strong young man of reasonably good appearance. The girls must have been flattered by his interest in them. He is a local as he knows the area like the back of his hand. He has a criminal record or has a history of violence towards women. Once we identify such men from the area, I suggest that we collect their DNA and fingerprints. Also, check their alibis. And try to be fast about this. If the killer comes to know about our plans, he might try to escape. I'll take the CP's help and get the necessary court orders so that you can collect the samples legally.'

'Yes, ma'am. You are right. In these villages, everybody knows everybody else and news of our investigation will spread like wildfire. We have to move fast.'

The ACP's face became stern. 'And there should be no more leaks about the investigation. Is that understood?'

Everybody's face became expressionless. Rao had been expecting a reprimand from the ACP on this matter. Constable Balakrishna, who was the one who had spoken to the reporter, assumed his most innocent expression.

The ACP continued. 'I don't know who in our team spoke to the paparazzi last time, but I will take harsher measures this time if there are any more leaks. Also, ensure that the villagers don't upload any more videos on social media like they did last time. Go to each house in the village and warn them. Tell them that strict action will be taken against them if anybody posts any fake or real news about the crime on social media.'

Rao nodded grimly. 'Yes, ma'am. Definitely, ma'am. I'll find out who leaked the information last time and deal with him severely.'

Balakrishna's heart raced, but he made sure his face didn't show any emotion. He really, really hoped that Rao wouldn't find out he had leaked the information to the reporters. He promised himself he'd never talk to a reporter again. He also pledged to invest considerable effort into the case, hoping to earn Rao's forgiveness swiftly if his involvement ever came to light.

Meanwhile, he quickly changed the topic. 'What I feel really happened was that this boy—Sunil—followed Renuka back to Deverakonda and then offered her a lift to the village; in this manner, he abducted her to the Tatte Bavi.'

Rao nodded solemnly. 'You could be right, Bala. Find out what this guy Sunil was doing when Renuka vanished. Also, get his DNA samples and try to match it with the DNA on the cigarette butts.'

---

28 April 2019

ADSP Bhujanga Rao, along with a team of constables, returned to Gazipur village the very next day and went to Renuka's home.

Renuka's father, Prakash, was sitting at the doorstep, looking glum. He brightened at the sight of Rao. 'Sir, have you found the killer?' He asked.

Rao shook his head glumly.

'Did you check on Sunil?' Prakash asked.

'We are going there now.'

'Yes, he had scratch marks on his face. Maybe Renuka struggled with him when he killed her.'

Rao nodded. 'Yes, I'll check.'

He went to meet Sunil along with a forensic technician. Sunil looked frightened on seeing Rao. But he readily provided his DNA sample. When asked about his scratches, he repeated the story that he had told Prakash. When asked if there were any witnesses to his fight, he nodded eagerly. He had several friends who would be willing to confirm what happened.

The police had DNA samples of the killer from Renuka's rape test kit. The samples collected from Sunil were immediately sent to the forensic lab to check if they matched. The police also went to Sunil's college, where his friends confirmed that he had got into a fight with a classmate named Manish. But the fight had happened after college, at about 3.00 p.m.

Rao called the ACP to update her. 'I think Sunil may not be involved in Renuka's murder. He really did get into a fight with one of his classmates.'

'Maybe he intentionally got into the fight to hide the fact that he got some scratches from Renuka? What time did he get into a fight?' She asked.

'About 3.00 p.m., ma'am.'

'Then he could have easily abducted Renuka at 12.30 p.m., committed the crime, hidden the body in a shallow grave and made it back to college, no?'

'Possible, ma'am,' Rao nodded. 'He has a bike. So it would take him about twenty-five minutes to get back to college. Suppose he abducted Renuka on the pretext of giving her a lift. He could have taken her to the Tatte Bavi, raped and killed her by 2.30 p.m. and then returned to college. Maybe that's why Renuka was buried in such a shallow grave. Probably, he didn't have enough time to dig a deeper grave.'

'Yes, anyway we will know for sure once the DNA sample reports come back, along with the match results,' the ACP said.

The police also started to do a door-to-door sample collection from all the men in the village. Some men had gone to Nalgonda for work. But the police managed to track down most of them and collected the DNA samples.

∽

3 May 2019

ADSP Rao had a review meeting with the ACP on 3 May 2019, where he updated her on the work done so far.

'We have sent all the DNA samples collected so far for forensic analysis.'

'What about this guy Sunil?'

'We don't know, ma'am. I have been following up with the forensic team, asking them to hurry up, but they are taking their own sweet time!' Rao was frustrated.

'Okay, I will personally follow up with the forensic team,' the ACP promised.

There was a small pause. Then the ACP said, 'Please check and double-check that all the DNA samples have been collected. This person might have slipped away from his home when he came to know that the police were collecting samples.'

'Yes, ma'am,' Rao said glumly. This investigation was turning out to be extreme hard work. 'I'll need a few more men to work on this case,' he told the ACP a bit hesitantly. More men meant more resources and an increased budget. But to his relief, the ACP supported him.

'Yes, of course. I'll immediately allocate a few more constables. This is a high-profile case and we have to solve it fast. Already a week has passed and there is no progress. The press is having a gala time maligning the police. The commissioner is under a lot of pressure. It seems that the MP of Nalgonda has been harassing him, demanding why there is no progress. And he, in turn, is asking me. And we have nothing to show despite the hard work we are putting in. We have to show some results soon, Rao!'

Rao said heatedly, 'But ma'am, we are working day and night, trying to solve this case. Going to all the villagers' homes, collecting DNA samples…'

'Sure, solid police work. But the problem is that the press doesn't understand how hard we are working. We have to show some results soon, Rao garu.'

'Sure, ma'am. But how?'

The ACP thought for some time. Then she said, 'As this killer is such a violent man, there must be some kind of criminal record. Or he might have a history of violence against his wife, if he is married, or against his sisters or girlfriend. Find out from the villagers if they are aware of any such person.'

6 May 2019

ADSP Bhujanga Rao went back to the village with ten constables, including Balakrishna. On seeing the police officer, a few more villagers gathered round eagerly.

Rao looked at them and said, 'Do any of the young men around here have criminal records?'

All of them shook their heads.

'This is a peaceful village, sir,' Prakash said. 'All the young men have either left home for higher studies or are gainfully employed in the town of Nalgonda.'

'What about Sunil?' Rao asked. Then he answered his own question, 'No... I don't think he has any criminal records in our police station.' Rao had been posted in the Nalgonda Police Staion for three years now and was acquainted with most of the habitual offenders. Then, another thought struck him. 'Has Sunil settled in this village recently?' Rao asked.

Prakash shook his head. 'No, sir. Sunil was born and brought up in this village only. I know him since he was a small child. He's kind of rowdy.'

One of the villagers spoke up in Sunil's defence. 'But I don't think that he has ever shown any criminal tendencies. He's just a boisterous person. Not a bad guy at heart. In fact,

I can't imagine him killing anybody!'

Prakash asked, disappointed, 'So there's no progress as of now?'

'I'm not at liberty to reveal anything when the investigation is in progress,' Rao said primly.

'What about Ramesh?' One of the villagers spoke up.

Prakash perked up. 'Yes, Ramesh has a criminal record. I had forgotten about him because I was convinced that Sunil killed my girl.'

Rao glanced sharply at the villager. 'Who is this Ramesh?'

'Sir, Ramesh Mudiraj is a mechanic. He works at a garage in the outskirts of the village. He has a bike and pesters local girls, offering them lifts. He used to work in Kurnool. But about a year back, he returned to the village. I've heard that he had a run-in with the police in Kurnool,' the villager told him.

'Where does this Ramesh stay?' Rao asked.

'He lives close to the Tatte Bavi. In fact, his father is part-owner of the well.'

ADSP Rao went to Ramesh's home. Unlike most other houses in the village, the door of this house was closed and locked from inside. This family appeared to be more prosperous than their neighbours, as the house was bigger and the courtyard well-tended. Rao could also see a garden at the back of the house, full of coconut and papaya trees.

He knocked on the door. A fat, elderly woman opened it. Rao guessed that she must be Ramesh's mother. The smell of mutton cooking wafted from inside. He could hear the hum of a pressure cooker in which the meat was cooking. The woman was wearing a thick gold chain and heavy gold bangles. Rao's impression that this was a prosperous household was reinforced.

Not wanting to arouse the woman's suspicion, Rao said mildly, 'You must have heard that a child named Renuka was murdered the day before yesterday in this village.'

A nervous tick suddenly started on the woman's left eyelid. She nodded mutely. Rao pretended not to notice her nervousness.

'Your name, ma?' He asked courteously.

'Varuna,' the woman mumbled nervously.

'We are questioning all the young men in this area. Are there any young men in this household?' Rao asked, opening his notebook.

The woman nodded. 'Yes. I have three sons, but they have all gone out. And my husband, of course,' she added as an afterthought.

Rao immediately discarded her husband as a suspect. Judging by Varuna's appearance, he guessed that her husband would be an elderly person. An elderly person wouldn't be able to commit this kind of crime.

'Can you give me the names of your sons?' Rao asked politely.

'Yes… S-Suresh, Ramesh and Rajesh Mudiraj.'

Rao noted down the names. 'How old are they? Where do they work?' He asked.

'Suresh is thirty years old. He works in Nalgonda as a peon. He and his wife live there,' the woman responded.

'What is Suresh's phone number?'

Varuna hesitated, then said, 'Please come inside. The numbers are noted down in my diary. I'll get it.'

The walls of the drawing room were painted blue, and had red-oxide flooring. An old-fashioned sofa was covered with a garish gold-printed cloth cover. A small, flat-screen TV was attached to the wall in front of the sofa. The pressure cooker suddenly whistled. Varuna gave a start as if startled by the sound.

Asking Rao to sit down, she switched on the fan and retreated inside. A fly was buzzing in the drawing room. It came and sat on Rao's hand. He swatted it away impatiently. Varuna's nervousness made him suspect that one of the sons could be involved in the girl's death. But he kept a poker face as he didn't want to alert her. Varuna returned with a tiny diary. She opened a page where Ramesh's and Suresh's names and phone numbers were written in Telugu.

Rao noted them down. 'What about Rajesh?'

'He goes to college. He's my youngest. Right now, he's gone to my mother's place for a visit as it is his summer holidays.' Varuna turned a page in her notebook. 'This is his phone number,' she said, extending the book to Rao so that he could note down the number.

'When did he go?'

'About twenty days back.'

'When will he be back?'

Varuna shrugged. 'He'll probably be back a week before his college restarts.'

'Did your sons provide DNA samples when the police did a door-to-door collection?'

Varuna shook her head. 'Well, Suresh stays in Nalgonda. Rajesh has gone to visit my mother, and Ramesh had gone away from Gazipur for two days when the police came for sample collection.'

'Where did he go?' Rao asked.

'He had gone to Kurnool as he had to appear for a court case.'

'What kind of court case?'

Varuna shook her head. 'I don't know exactly. Ramesh was working as a car mechanic in Kurnool. The owner of the workshop accused him of stealing money and filed a police complaint against him. Now the case is in court and he has to regularly go to Kurnool for that. But Ramesh told me that he had not stolen any money and that his former employer had wrongfully accused him.'

'Do you believe Ramesh?' Rao asked.

'Of course, sir. My Ramesh is not a thief. We have enough money. He has no need to steal,' Varuna said proudly and defiantly.

'Where is Ramesh now?' Rao asked casually, though this was the question he had been itching to ask all along.

'Ramesh has gone out,' Varuna said.

'Do you know where?'

Varuna shook her head. 'He said something about going to the garage where he works as there was some extra work that he needed to do.'

'Where is this garage?'

'He works in a small workshop called Royal Garage.'

'Oh, that garage in Deverakonda?' The police often got their bikes repaired there.

'Yes,' Varuna nodded. 'He works there as a mechanic.'

Rao paused deliberately. Though Varuna had initially been nervous, she had overcome her nervousness in the course of their conversation. He wanted her to feel the tension again. He knew that the deliberate pause would trigger that tension in Varuna. It was a technique that Rao often used to make the person he was interrogating nervous.

His trick worked as Varuna suddenly started to fidget and, as if to break the awkward silence, offered him a glass of water, which Rao politely declined.

'Are you suspecting my sons?' Varuna asked, nervously wringing her hands. As Rao didn't respond immediately, she went on. 'They are good boys. They have nothing to do with Renuka's disappearance.' She was visibly trembling now.

'No need to worry, ma,' Rao said reassuringly. 'This is just a routine enquiry.'

Taking his leave, Rao went straight to the Royal Garage.

But to his disappointment, the garage was closed. He set about trying to trace the owner of the garage, Lateef, who lived in Deverakonda. When he finally tracked down Lateef in his home, Rao was feeling hot and irritable. Testily, he demanded to know why the garage was closed. Lateef nervously responded that the garage remained closed every Monday. Rao asked irritably where Ramesh was. Lateef responded that he had no idea where Ramesh was, but he could try to call him. Lateef tried calling Ramesh's mobile number but his phone was switched off.

Rao felt disappointed. But there was nothing he could do. He ordered a police informer from the village to monitor Ramesh's home. The informer was instructed to call Rao as soon as Ramesh returned home.

Returning to his office, Rao was happy to note that Renuka's autopsy report had come in by email. The report said that the girl had been raped and then strangled. Her spine was broken and there was an injury mark on her chest, possibly as a result of a fall from a height. According to the autopsy report, the girl was alive when she was raped as there was blood under her fingernails, possibly from scratching the rapist as she struggled with him.

Rao called the forensic team. The forensic doctor confirmed that he had been able to collect the DNA of the rapist from the vaginal swabs. Rao was particularly disappointed when the analyst told him that Sunil's DNA didn't match the DNA from the rape test kit.

Rao immediately called the ACP. 'Ma'am, the autopsy report has come in. The girl was raped and strangled. She was buried in the well after that. A very violent and brutal death. We have collected evidence through the rape test kit. The only thing that remains to be done is to find the person whose DNA matches this sample.'

'What about Sunil?' The ACP asked.

Rao sighed. 'Unfortunately, it's not a match. He didn't do it.'

'What about the other samples?'

'No match as of now. But we had missed all the men in one particular family. And I particularly suspect the second son of this family, a young man named Ramesh. A person in the village told me that Ramesh was involved in some criminal case in Kurnool. He is the only one who matches our profile as of now. But I have not been able to collect his DNA sample as I have been unable to trace him.'

'Okay, great job. Call the Kurnool police and find out about the case in which this Ramesh was involved.'

'I'll do that, ma'am.'

Rao called the Kurnool police. They informed him that Ramesh and four of his friends were suspects in the murder of a prostitute in Kurnool in 2017. Rao got goosebumps when the inspector at the other end said, 'Ramesh is the main suspect in the murder. A local witness says that the prostitute, who was a minor, was arguing with him. It seems that he and his friends had sex with her but were refusing to pay. They were all drunk. He distinctly heard Ramesh threatening to kill her and bury her in a nearby pond. The witness didn't think that they were serious. But the prostitute vanished and her father, who was also her pimp, complained to us. Then a few days later, a dead body was found floating in the pond close to where the witness had seen the prostitute arguing with the men. Somebody had strangled her and tied her down with a heavy stone and thrown her into the pond. But the body had bloated and the gas had caused the body to float. The autopsy results showed that the girl had been alive when she was drowned.

There was water in her lungs. From the condition of her genitals, she was also most probably raped. But the DNA evidence was, of course, washed away by the water.'

Rao called the ACP again and updated her.

'Great job, Rao garu. Looks like Ramesh is our man. But this time he was unlucky. The well in which he buried Renuka's body was dry and we have his DNA. The question is, does Ramesh's mother really not know that he was involved in a murder case in Kurnool? I think she knows and was trying her best to throw you off track.'

༄

6 May 2019; 11.00 p.m.; Ramesh's Home

The living room was dimly lit and Varuna sat anxiously on the sofa waiting for Ramesh. A woman was reading the news in Telugu on TV. Renuka's murder has become big news. The news channels were talking about nothing else. A juicy murder case involving a possible serial killer always fetched good TRPs. She listened anxiously, but very little information was available. Only that a skeleton and a dead body had been found buried in Tatte Bavi, and the police suspected that it was the work of a serial killer. The report was quite critical of the Telangana Police, implying that they were too lax and the culprit should have been caught by now. Venkat, Ramesh's father, a thin, weather-beaten man, sat nearby, also watching the news. He was concerned and disgusted.

Ramesh staggered in, drunk. He smelled of cheap alcohol and cigarettes. He ignored his parents and lurched towards his small bedroom.

Varuna asked sharply, 'Ramesh, where have you been? It's late, and I've been so worried. I have kept dinner ready for you.'

'Don't want to eat,' Ramesh slurred.

'Have you been drinking again?' Varuna asked sternly.

Ramesh glared at his mother. 'Mind your own business, amma! I don't need your nagging!'

Venkat cleared his throat. He wanted to intervene but wasn't sure how to approach the situation. He said, 'Ramesh, calm down. Your mother's just worried about you.'

Ramesh glanced angrily at his father. He slurred, 'Hey, who the hell are you to tell me to calm down, madarchod? You stay out of this! I don't want any *gyaanam* from you; I have heard enough of your lectures.'

Venkat flinched at his son's harsh words, but he tried to stay calm and continued in a mild tone, 'Look, Ramesh, I know I haven't been the best father. But you need to understand…'

Ramesh didn't allow Venkat to finish speaking, 'Understand what? That you were a monster to me when I was a kid?' He swayed, nearly falling down, and clutched the wall for support.

Varuna looked on, heartbroken by the tension between father and son. She said tearfully, 'Please stop, both of you. Let's not fight now.'

Ramesh glared at his mother. 'You shut up! Why didn't

Candle in the Wind

you stop him when he used to beat the shit out of me when I was a small, helpless child? You always supported him. I hate you!'

Varuna looked away, unable to meet Ramesh's gaze. She said defiantly, 'I supported your father because I thought he could beat some good sense into you. You were such a naughty child. Your teachers used to constantly complain about you, accusing you of cheating during exams and bullying other kids.'

Ramesh said bitterly, 'Of course you believed the teachers and not your own son! Father used to beat me inhumanely. He beat me so hard sometimes that I lost consciousness. You never cared about me. It was only Suresh you cared about. Suresh is so good,' he said, mimicking his mother. 'Why can't you be like him? Well, what is he doing now? He married and ran away from home with his wife. He hardly even calls you. Now he works as a peon. I earn a lot more money! Even then, you don't give a fuck about me!'

'Ramesh, please don't let anger consume you. We're a family and we need to stick together,' Varuna pleaded.

Ramesh looked down contemptuously at both of them. 'A family? There's no family here. Just pain and regret.'

Varuna let out a frustrated sigh. She reached out to Ramesh, and ran her hand through his hair, trying to comfort him. 'Okay, I'm saying sorry on behalf of both of us. Please calm down.' As Ramesh seemed to cool down a bit, she said in a trembling voice, 'Ramesh, the police came looking for you today! That's why we are waiting up.

I wanted to tell you right away. I called you, but your mobile number was switched off.'

Ramesh sobered up in a hurry. 'The police!'

Varuna said unsteadily, 'Ramesh, they wanted to question you about that girl, Renuka.'

Ramesh's face contorted with rage and he clenched his fists. 'What do those madarchods want from me? Aren't they happy enough harassing me for nothing in Kurnool? I didn't do anything to this girl!'

Venkat asked, 'Are you telling me the truth, Ramesh? Are you involved in her death?'

Ramesh looked away, unable to meet his father's gaze. He said, a bit defensively, 'No! Why can't you believe me for a change?'

'Because the Kurnool police are also looking for you, Ramesh,' Venkat snapped. 'You can't go on like this!'

Ramesh's frustration reached its peak and he shouted, 'The Kurnool police are unnecessarily harassing me. I had nothing to do with that prostitute's death. I didn't do it! You think I am some kind of monster, don't you?' He sighed in frustration.

Varuna said softly, 'No, Ramesh, you're my son. I love you! If you say you didn't do anything wrong, I believe you.'

Ramesh's emotions were in a turmoil as he looked at his parents. He stumbled closer to Varuna, his anger mixed with sadness. 'You don't understand anything, amma! Life has never been fair to me! Now, if you leave me alone, I would like to go to bed. I'll go and meet that fucking policeman tomorrow. I'll give him a piece of my mind.

Coming and harassing me like this!'

There was a sudden knock on their front door. All of them froze as a voice outside said loudly, 'Police! Open the door.' It was Rao, who had rushed to Ramesh's home after the informer had called to tell him that Ramesh was back home. They arrested him on the spot, and confiscated his wallet and mobile phone. There was no charge on his phone, which is why neither his mother nor the police had been able to contact him.

---

7 May 2019

ADSP Bhujanga Rao and Constable Bheem entered the lockup where Ramesh was the sole prisoner. The dimly lit room with a naked lightbulb was shabby with peeling paint. Ramesh cowered on the floor in a corner of the room. Dirty and unkempt, he stank of alcohol.

Rao exuded an aura of authority and intimidation as he went on the offensive, 'Why was your mobile switched off yesterday? Where were you?'

'S-sir, I was nearby only. At a friend's house.'

Bheem slapped him hard. The sound reverberated across the cell. 'Tell us the truth, chutiya! Why was your phone switched off? Were you raping and killing another girl and didn't want to be disturbed?'

'S-sir, I had gone to visit a girlfriend in Pattharghat.'

Pattharghat was a notable red-light area near Nalgonda. 'Then I went to a bar and got drunk. I never noticed that the battery of my phone had died. Sir, you can ask Mallika and the bar owner.'

'You thought you were smart, didn't you, Ramesh? You killed innocent girls and hid their bodies in the well. But we aren't fools. We know that it was you.'

Ramesh peered at Rao from the corner of his eyes, his hands over his head as if he was expecting a blow at any moment. 'I didn't do anything, saab,' he stammered. 'You have the wrong person.'

Rao smirked. 'Oh, we have more than enough evidence to put you away for good. We found a witness who saw you coming out of that well where we exhumed the girl's body,' he lied smoothly.

Ramesh had faced police interrogation before, in Kurnool. He wasn't fooled by this lie. In any case, he was a tough cookie. He decided to brazen it out. He said earnestly, 'That's impossible, sir. I wasn't there at all.'

'We found Renuka's school ID card in your wallet. Why was her ID card in your wallet, Ramesh?'

Ramesh's heart skipped a beat. He had forgotten about the ID card. 'I-I found the ID card on the road between Deverakonda and Gazipur. I was planning to return the card to her father,' he stammered.

'So you knew the girl.'

'Sir, Gazipur is a small village. Everybody knows everybody else.'

'Hmm... So why didn't you return the card?'

'S-saab, by that time, I heard that the girl had died. I was scared that the police would think that I had committed the crime.'

'I don't believe you,' Rao said flatly. 'You murdered the girl and dumped her body in the well.'

'No sir, I didn't do anything.'

Bheem slapped Ramesh so hard that blood spurted from Ramesh's nose. 'Tell us the truth! Madarchod!' He snarled.

Ramesh wiped the blood on his nose with his hands. Internally, he was burning with rage. If he ever got out, he would show this constable what stuff he was made of, he promised himself.

Outwardly, he pretended to cower in fear. 'I didn't do anything,' he whined.

Rao leaned forward and glared at Ramesh. He spat on Ramesh's face. 'We checked the browsing history on your phone, madarchod! You enjoy violent porn. Young girls, not even teenagers, being raped and beaten up. My God! You are insane!'

Ramesh looked at Rao impassively. He didn't know what browsing history was. But he guessed that somehow the police had found out about his addiction to violent porn. He said, 'I don't watch such things. I have a friend who borrows my phone and watches them.' He swerved his face and Bheem's fist narrowly missed him. 'S-saab, please believe me. I'm not lying.'

Rao leaned in closer, his eyes locked on Ramesh. 'You raped and killed Renuka. We have more than just a witness.

Your DNA is all over that girl's body, Ramesh. I'm sure that it is your DNA there.'

'DNA? What's that? I have nothing to do with her death, sir! Please believe me.' He clutched at Rao's feet. 'Sir, I'm a poor farmer's son. Please don't pin this on me. I didn't know whose body that was and you wouldn't find anything connecting me to it.'

Rao kicked Ramesh in disgust. 'Don't touch me, madarchod! You have killed these innocent girls. I have no doubt about it.'

He gestured to a forensic technician who had been standing outside, nervously observing the scene. 'Take this man's blood sample and fingerprint him.'

Ramesh wriggled and fought against his sample being taken forcibly, but Bheem, who was a strong and muscular young man, overpowered him easily. Bheem slapped Ramesh so hard that the sound could be heard two rooms away. The pathologist, a mild-mannered man, shuddered. Ramesh cowered in fear against the wall. Bheem asked the pathologist to get on with his job. With the help of a syringe, the pathologist took a sample of Ramesh's venous blood, and collected it in a purple stoppered vacutainer.

After the sample was taken, Rao said, 'We know that you killed the two girls, madarchod. When the DNA results come back—and they match—you will be begging for mercy.'

Ramesh was still dazed by the slap. He had no idea what DNA was or what Rao was talking about. He suspected that the police might have found traces of his sperm on the dead girl, but how would they match his blood with the sperm? He had a strong suspicion that the policeman was being dishonest, attempting to coerce a confession from him. However, he was resolute in refusing to confess. Despite his earlier act of pretending to be severely injured and on the verge of collapsing when Bheem had beaten him, he was prepared to endure any level of physical punishment.

Once the pathologist had left, Rao asked harshly, 'What about the prostitute you killed in Kurnool?'

Ramesh's eyes widened, but he quickly regained his composure. 'I have no idea what you are talking about, saab.'

'Oh, we know that the Kurnool Police has been after you on a similar case. A young girl—an underage prostitute—was strangled and drowned in a pond, weighed down with stone, in Kurnool a year back, while you were working there. Sound familiar?'

Ramesh looked at Rao through the corner of his eyes like a petty thief. 'I know nothing about that. You can't tie me to that crime,' he whined.

Rao leaned in, a predatory glint in his eyes. 'Know nothing, huh? You can try to deny your involvement all you want, but the evidence doesn't lie. We are building a solid case against you, and it's only a matter of time before we bring you to justice for all your heinous acts. We will prove everything, Ramesh. Your reign of terror is over. And when we are done with you, you'll never see the light of day again.'

But Ramesh seemed unfazed by Rao's threat. He continued to deny any involvement in Renuka's murder.

Even though Constable Bheem slapped Ramesh very hard a few more times, they were unable to extract a confession from him.

After Rao came out of the lockup room, he called the forensic lab. 'I want the reports as soon as possible,' he told them. 'I'll get ACP ma'am to send an email to the forensic head explaining the urgency of the situation. We are dealing with a serial killer here,' he said.

∽

The next day, ADSP Rao got another breakthrough when a man named Nagaraju came to meet him at 10.00 a.m. Rao liked Nagaraju. He was the husband of the village sarpanch and was on good terms with the police.

'Arrey, Nagaraju garu. Long time! Come, come. Want to have some tea?'

Nagaraju smiled and accepted the offer. Rao sent for a constable and asked him to get tea and onion samosas from the nearby stall.

'Tell me. What has brought you here so early in the morning?'

'I heard that Renuka's body was found buried in the Tatte Bavi?' Nagaraju asked.

'Yes, on 26 April. How come you got the news so late?'

'I had gone to Kukatpally to visit some relatives on the 25th. When I came back late last night, the wifey told me about Renuka's murder. I know Renuka's family well. Renuka was a good girl. Excellent in her studies. She wanted to be a doctor and was her mother's pet. I hear that the mother is nearly insane with grief.' He sighed, then said, 'But the reason I came to meet you is, I saw her that day on the outskirts of Gazipur, coming back from school. Ramesh, the mechanic, was giving her a lift to the village on his bike.'

Rao felt elated. Now there was no doubt in his mind. Ramesh was the person last seen with the victim. Rao itched to get his hands on the forensic report. He was now 99 per cent sure that Ramesh was the killer.

The report came back a few days later, on 10 May. The results were a match. Ramesh was finally trapped. Rao called the ACP to give her the good news.

∽

The police formally arrested Ramesh after the DNA evidence matched, and incarcerated him in the Chanchalguda Jail after he was denied bail due to the grave nature of his crimes. His fingerprints had been found on Renuka's school bag.

The ACP wanted to explain to Ramesh how his guilt had been proven beyond a reasonable doubt by using the DNA testing technique. The reasoning behind this was that she wanted to convince him that he would no longer get away by denying the truth. The ultimate aim of the ACP was to get Ramesh to confess to his crime so as to reconstruct the crime scene with his help. She also wanted to understand why Ramesh had committed, these crimes.

I Will Never Let You Go

Ramesh was brought into the warden's office. He was handcuffed and a burly police officer was standing guard with a loaded gun, ready to shoot if Ramesh stirred up trouble. The ACP looked Ramesh in the eye and said, 'You know why you have been convicted, don't you? We found DNA evidence at the crime scene, and it matches yours.'

Ramesh's eyes widened with surprise, and he scratched his head, clearly puzzled. 'What do you mean, DNA? How can you match that with me? I don't even know what DNA is!' He blurted out. The ACP could see genuine confusion on Ramesh's face, and she realized that Ramesh had no understanding of modern forensic techniques. Taking a moment to gather her thoughts, the ACP decided to explain it in a manner even a child could understand.

'Alright Ramesh, let me break it down for you,' she began patiently. 'DNA is like a unique code that's inside all of us. It's passed down from our parents and makes us who we are. Every person has their own distinct DNA code, like a fingerprint. It's found in our hair, skin, blood and other bodily fluids. You left your DNA inside Renuka when you raped her. The same DNA is also available in your blood, and in the blood sample that we collected from you.'

Ramesh squinted. 'So, you're saying you found this "DNA code" at the crime scene and it matches mine?' He asked, still trying to understand the concept.

The ACP nodded. 'Yes, that's right. You are guilty according to science and no lawyer in the world would be able to prove otherwise.'

Candle in the Wind

Ramesh's eyes darted around the room, surprised that something as seemingly unimportant as his blood could link him to the crime. He had never imagined that such a thing was possible.

'Now Ramesh, we know that you have no lawyer, and you told the warden that you have no money to appoint one. Is that correct?'

Ramesh looked at his feet and nodded mutely. His family had disowned him once they came to know about the crimes he had committed.

The ACP rubbed her hands briskly and said, 'Okay. We will help you to get a defence lawyer appointed by the government, but only if you help us reconstruct the crime scenes and confess to all the murders that you have committed.'

Ramesh again nodded mutely. He was still in a state of shock over how easily the police had caught him. He had become complacent after committing the murders in that area and thought of himself as invincible. The fact that his blood sample could be used to prove that he had raped those *kannagattalu*—those sluts—was still surreal to him despite the ACP's explanation. The ACP had grappled with the ethics of granting a ruthless killer the opportunity to revisit the places of his monstrous acts. Nevertheless, she saw a potential opportunity to get an insight into a serial killer's psyche and modus operandi, which could aid in solving other cases and identifying possible accomplices.

The process began with meticulous planning. Rao and his team ensured that there was total secrecy about the entire business, so there were no unnecessary crowds. They were afraid that the villagers would lynch Ramesh if they got their hands on him.

At the crack of dawn, under heavy police guard, Ramesh was transported to the Tatte Bavi and Marri Bavi wells. As they arrived at each crime scene, the atmosphere was laden with tension. As they approached each location, Ramesh would recount the events leading up to the crime, sometimes with a detached demeanour and at other times with unsettling enthusiasm. He would walk the investigators through his actions—step by step—recounting his sinister thoughts and emotions as he committed each murder.

He led the police to another grave inside the Marri Bavi where he had raped and killed an eleven-year-old girl. The girl had come to Gazipur village to visit her aunt and was on her way back home to Nalgonda. Ramesh had offered her a lift and she had accepted. Ramesh took her to an isolated place close to the Marri Bavi and attempted to rape her. But she started to scream and, in the struggle, he accidently smothered the girl to death. When he realized what he had done, he got hold of a bag of fertilizer from a nearby field, put the girl inside the bag and drove his bike to the Marri Bavi, where he buried her. He said that the girl had told him that her name was Sumeeta. He buried this body quite deep as the mud at the bottom was still wet and easy to scoop out. That was the reason the police didn't discover her grave when they climbed into the well to collect Renuka's school bag. The police now dug at the spot Ramesh indicated and discovered the skeleton of the eleven-year-old girl.

This was his first murder in that area. DNA evidence taken from the skeleton proved that Ramesh was telling the truth. Sumeeta's father had lodged a missing person's complaint in the Nalgonda Police Station two years back, but the case had remained unsolved.

Ramesh had killed Swapna, his second murder in that area, eight months back. He had carefully selected his target at that time. He knew nobody in Swapna's family cared for her, so no one would look for her if she disappeared. He had seen her walking towards the outskirts of Gazipur one day and realized she was going to college. He had followed her on his bike and offered her a ride. Swapna knew Ramesh and didn't particularly like him because of his drinking habits. But she was late for class, and had accepted the lift as it would save her a one-kilometre walk. On the way, he stopped near Tatte Bhavi. As he had anticipated, there was nobody around.

'I need to take a leak,' he said.

Then he waited in the bushes and stealthily watched her. When he noticed that she was getting fidgety, he let out a strangled shout, 'Help!'

'What happened?' Swapna rushed over in concern, thinking he had hurt himself.

He had grabbed her then, and tried to pull her clothes off. But she was surprisingly strong and started to scream. He put his hands over her mouth to stop her from screaming, but she bit him hard. Blood spurted from his hand and the rage that always simmered within him rose to the surface. He slammed his fist into her stomach. Swapna doubled over and gasped for breath, unable to scream. He then lifted her and threw her down the forty-six-feet well. He heard the *thud* of the body and leaned over the edge. Peering in, he could see her moving feebly. He hid his bike under some bushes and climbed inside.

As she lay at the bottom of the well in intense pain, gasping for breath and unable to move, he raped her—staring into her eyes as she died. He had heard her death rattle and climaxed. At that moment, he had felt like God—all-powerful! He could bring death to anybody at any time. After a while, he had sex with her body once more. He had never felt happier. Then he dressed the body, retrieved her bag—which was lying next to the mouth of the well—and buried it inside, along with her body.

His urge to kill was temporarily satiated. However, within a few months, the compulsion resurfaced and started to grow. He searched hard for other victims, but couldn't find anybody suitable. He was getting desperate by the time he spotted Renuka under the tamarind tree in Deverakonda. He knew that Renuka would be missed immediately. But his patience was wearing thin and his confidence had grown, having gotten away with three murders by then—one in Kurnool and two in Gazipur. The Nalgonda Police were dumb. They would never find him. He offered Renuka a lift. They would have to pass the Tatte Bavi on the way to her home.

The chilling details revealed during these reconstructions were a harrowing testament to the extent of Ramesh's depravity. He spoke matter-of-factly about the terror he instilled in his victims, the pain he inflicted upon them, and the satisfaction he derived from their helplessness. His face was devoid of any emotion as he described how he had thrown Renuka down the Tatte Bavi in exactly the same way as he had thrown down Swapna, after she resisted his advances and tried to scream; how she had still been alive, but was unable to move; how she had watched helplessly as he climbed down the well, undressed her and then raped her; how she had been alive even after this ordeal; how he had strangled her with her dupatta and then—as it was too hot to do any digging—simply piled her clothes on top of her naked body and thrown mud and gravel over it. Once he climbed back to the surface, he realized that her school bag was still lying near the well. So he searched it to see if there was an ID card. He found her ID card, kept it in his wallet, and hidden the bag in some bushes behind the Tatte Bavi. Then he had gone to an alcohol shop where he bought beer and cigarettes. It was while drinking beer beneath the shade of a neem tree near the Marri Bavi that he realized that some stray animal might drag the bag out. So he had gone back to Tatte Bavi, collected Renuka's bag and threw it into the Marri Bavi well. When asked why he had thrown the bag in the Marri Bavi well while he had buried the body in the Tatte Bavi, he said that he thought Marri Bavi would be a better hiding place as even if somebody spotted the bag, they wouldn't know where the body was. The ACP's prediction as to why the body and bag were in two different wells had proved to be chillingly true. Ramesh seemed to regret his laziness in not burying the school bag, as Senthil's sharp eyes had spotted it when he looked into the well while searching for Renuka. When the ACP asked why he had kept the ID card, Ramesh said that he wanted to remember how she had died in his hands, and the photo in her ID card helped him revisit the crime in his mind, giving him the desired high. He confessed that killing the girls had given him great pleasure. He also confessed to murdering the prostitute in Kurnool.

What deeply disturbed the ACP was the way Ramesh explained all his gruesome deeds in an unemotional, matter-of-fact voice, as if he were discussing something as mundane as what he had eaten for breakfast. When asked why he committed these heinous crimes, he had no answer. The ACP realized that Ramesh himself had no idea why he had done what he had.

Finally, Ramesh's crime scene reconstructions provided chilling insight into a serial killer's mindset. So many innocent lives were lost—and their families shattered—because of him and his disgusting need to satisfy his animal urges. The reconstructions are a haunting testament to the darkest depths of the human psyche to which people can descend.

∞

At a high-level meeting with the Crimes & SIT team, the ACP said, 'This monster has to pay for his crimes. The girls and their families deserve justice.'

Rao agreed with a nod. 'We have gathered enough

evidence to prove the charges. There should be no doubt whatsoever in this case.'

With a strong case built for the prosecution, the ACP went to a packed press conference. 'Today, I stand here with a heavy heart, but with the determination to get justice for the innocent victims of these heinous crimes,' she said with conviction in her voice. The reporters surrounded her and bombarded her with questions, which the ACP answered calmly and confidently, telling the public that the law will take its course and justice will be done.

The trial commenced, and the courtroom was filled with tension. Ramesh's court-appointed defence lawyer half-heartedly tried to argue for leniency. But even he was disgusted by the crimes committed by Ramesh. The evidence presented to the prosecutor by the ACP and Rao left no room for doubt. The testimonies of the old lady, who had seen Renuka coming back from school, and the sarpanch's husband, who had seen Renuka riding pillion on Ramesh's bike just before she was murdered, further solidified the case against him.

In the end, the court delivered its verdict. 'Ramesh, for the crimes you have committed, the court hereby sentences you to death,' the judge pronounced.

Thanks to the relentless pursuit of justice by the ACP, ADSP Bhujanga Rao, and the entire investigation team, the village of Gazipur found closure. The memory of Renuka, Madhavi and Swapna lives on as a testament to the need for unyielding determination in the face of darkness.

But the shadow of the events still lingers over the region. The villagers claim that the Marri Bavi and Tatte Bavi are haunted, and nobody ever goes there after dark.

www.ingramcontent.com/pod-product-compliance
Lightning Source LLC
Chambersburg PA
CBHW032127160426
43197CB00008B/548